D0948312

What people are saying about Revolutionary Agreements . . .

A great book! *Revolutionary Agreements* is a series of powerful and profound life messages that can open up a world of possibilities for you.
— *Brian Tracy, author,* Million Dollar Habits

Revolutionary Agreements line up like a stairway to a better life . . . each step will raise your level of awareness, enabling you to see the greatness that has been placed in your marvelous mind. Read it, then internalize it . . . your reward will be well worth the time and effort invested.
— *Bob Proctor, author,* You Were Born Rich

What's so "revolutionary" about *Revolutionary Agreements* is its head-heart connection. It is a profound collection of practical things to *do* about who and how to *be* to be all we desire, dream and deserve.
— *John Milton Fogg, author,* The Greatest Networker in the World

Revolutionary Agreements brings our minds, hearts and relationships to full attention. Tune into Marian Head's strategies and your human instrument will sing a clearer and stronger song with the world. Read and resonate!
— *Don Campbell, musician, lecturer, author,* The Mozart Effect

If you're serious about personal growth, you're going to love *Revolutionary Agreements*. Study them, experience them, and watch your life change. I highly recommend it.
— *Larry Wilson, Founder, Wilson Learning, author,* One-Minute Salesperson

Revolutionary Agreements is a wonderful guide to a fulfilling and loving life. It takes the great movements for peace and justice of the '60s and translates that impulse into sustainable action to transform ourselves and society. It will empower millions of us to model the change we want to see in the world.
— *Barbara Marx Hubbard, President, Foundation for Conscious Evolution, first woman nominee for Vice President of the United States (1984 Democratic National Convention)*

Marian Head's vision and organizational brilliance made it possible to manifest the historic Soviet-American Citizens' Summits (1988 and 1990) that Soviet and Russian officials have hailed as turning points in ending cold war stereotypes. The *Revolutionary Agreements* played a central role in building relationships and strengthening communication among my team members during these momentous events. Thank you, Marian! The work you're doing brings hope to the world.

— *Rama Vernon, President, Center for International Dialogue, Founder, Women of Vision in Action (WOVA) and The International Peace College, Co-founder,* Yoga Journal

Marian Head shares her life's lessons from the heart. Read and learn about building greatness in life.

— *David Neenan, Founder and President, Neenan Company*

You absolutely have a winner on your hands. It is simple and direct, it reads easily, from the heart, and rings true. And for most of life, I have found the simplest things are usually those that are incorporated and endure. This is the instruction book many people are hungry for. Such a gift it will become for millions.

— *Gale Arnold, former Director, International Alliance of Social Architects*

John Lennon dared us to "imagine." Marian Head took him seriously and did something about it: she wrote *Revolutionary Agreements* . . . the ultimate handbook for change, a powerful template for changing the way we relate to one another. A remarkable, groundbreaking effort!

— *Chris Gross, CEO, Gabriel Media Group*

A true test of the effectiveness of a book of this nature is how it plays out in the life of the author. As Chairperson of our Associate Council, Marian has collaborated with me on many sensitive and sometimes controversial issues, yet even when our beliefs differed she was always able to walk her talk. It is through those experiences that I can say *Revolutionary Agreements* is a work from her heart, with underlying principles that are useful and timeless.

— *Sam Caster, Chairman and CEO, Mannatech Incorporated*

Revolutionary Agreements is a deceptively simple and incredibly powerful guide to living a richer, deeper and more satisfying life. As someone who has lived and worked with these Agreements for over 20 years, I am thrilled that Marian is offering her stories as a model of success and happiness in such a personal and accessible way. Incorporating any one of these Agreements into your life leads to tremendous growth.

— *Laurie Weiss, Ph.D., author,* What is the Emperor Wearing?
  Truth-Telling in Business Relationships

It's clean, it's fresh, and it has no pretense. Marian Head shares a simple, straightforward, powerful message that is applicable in everyday practical living—and she shares it straight from her heart to the reader's heart. To borrow from Walt Whitman, ". . . This is not just a book. Who touches this, touches a person."

— *Nick Gordon, international speaker, life coach*

Revolutionary Agreements offers easy-to-implement tools destined to help individuals and communities work and play from conscious choice. Marian Head's words both excite and inspire us to create internal and external positive change.

— *Heather Ash, author,* The Four Elements of Change

I am grateful to Marian Head for bringing the *Revolutionary Agreements* to others, at home, at work, in relationships, among friends, clubs, and wherever two or more are gathered. Marian's personal testimony illustrates the power that is unleashed when we work together for the good of all. The *Revolutionary Agreements* have changed lives, transformed businesses, and improved communities . . . It is an idea whose time has come.
— *Ward Flynn, author,* The Truth Zone: Building the Truthful Organization from the Bottom Up!

Life is as simple and as rewarding as we make it. And it doesn't get any simpler or more rewarding than when we live it to its fullest, guided by the intelligence and wisdom of the *Revolutionary Agreements*! Read them and ride the wave to the glorious future that waits for you.
— *Linda M. Lopeke, author,* Extreme Self-Esteem

As I read this book I thought of so many people I would love to give it to. *Revolutionary Agreements* is brilliantly written, very moving and *important*. This is what the world desperately needs as we attempt to find sanity and create community during these challenging times.
— *Marion Culhane, Co-founder, Global Family, entrepreneur and life coach*

REVOLUTIONARY AGREEMENTS

TRUTH

ACCEPTANCE

GRATITUDE

Marian Head

First Hardcover Edition, March 2005

Cover design by Gregg Lauer, www.creatf.com
Editing by John David Mann, www.johndavidmann.com
Printed in the United States of America

ISBN 0-9759796-3-9
Library of Congress Control Number: 2004114941

PO Box 1113
Niwot, Colorado 80544-1113
www.MarlinPress.com

10 9 8 7 6 5 4 3 2 1   05   06   07   08

To Peace within us all,
that we may know
Peace on Earth.

Revolutionary

Bringing about a major or fundamental change of paradigm, or in the way of thinking about or visualizing something.*

Evolution

A process of gradual and relatively peaceful social, political and economic advance. Growth. Unfolding.*

Agreement

Harmony of opinion, action or character. An arrangement as to a course of action.*

* *Merriam Webster's Collegiate Dictionary*, Tenth Edition

$\mathscr{I}$NVITATION

The world works by agreements, whether spoken or unspoken, conscious or not. We all have agreements: agreements with our co-workers, with our spouses, siblings, parents and children, with people we know and even those we don't. Perhaps most importantly, we have agreements with ourselves.

Twenty years ago, I consciously began using a specific set of agreements to guide my daily actions with family, friends and co-workers. During that time I've changed, and in the process my world seems to have changed as well. As unnecessary drama in my life gave way to greater inner peace, the world became a more loving place in which to live.

Have I truly changed the world around me? Or is it simply that, like the caterpillar turned butterfly, I now have a different perspective? I cannot say for sure. Either way, since adopting these Agreements I have created a more satisfying life, replacing unwanted stress, struggle and suffering with greater emotional freedom, joy and fulfillment.

From the very depths of my heart, I invite you to adopt these Agreements as your own and join me in this Revolution—and in so doing, to transform your life and your world.

You must be the change you wish to see in the world.
—Mahatma Gandhi

Marian Head
Kapaa, Kauai
January 2005

CONTENTS

$\mathcal{A}$CKNOWLEDGMENTS

I am thankful for this opportunity to share in writing the deep gratitude I have for a lifetime of unconditional love and support from my family.

My father (we called him "honest Abe") is my spiritual mentor. He demonstrated a loving life under the harshest of circumstances; reveled in and honored the gifts of nature; and exemplified truth, acceptance and gratitude as though he were their author. He believed in me.

My mother Ann is always there for me, with both her sharp mind and kind heart. Her oft-repeated delight in me from my birth ("You were born with a smile on your face!") has given me the courage and inspiration to live up to who I am.

My brother Stephen has given me plenty of grist for the mill: lots of life lessons from the dog-and-cat interactions of siblings. I am grateful for the depth and respect of our recent loving connection and for the special role he plays as "intended audience" for this book.

I would need an entire book to thank my husband Glenn for all that he gives to me and to life. Glenn is my polar opposite: to my driven nature, he is a sweet resting place; to my fiery hot passion, he is my Buddha; to my dramatic responses to life, he is the inner peace I so admire. Whether my wish of the moment was to be president of a nation or to sit on a rock and admire the sky, my dear Glenn would support me unconditionally and say, "Whatever makes your heart sing."

I am a grateful admirer of my finest teacher, my teenage son Michael. His zest for life uplifts all in his path and is always a welcome reminder for me to "lighten up."

Thank goodness this is the first book in a series! I will need the many pages of future books to adequately thank all those who gift me and this work with their love, inspiration, encouragement and expertise. I will name a few of them here:

Gale Arnold, for her loving insistence that I get this book out of my computer and into the hands of readers.

Chris and Josephine Gross, for allowing me to write for their journal, *Networking Times*, and to learn that I could actually do so; and for their introduction to their Editor in Chief, John David Mann, who partnered with me in bringing this book to life through his magnificent wordsmithing.

My friend A.J. Grant, for her gracious time, compassion and expertise, which lifted my manuscript out of the dust and set me on the path to completing this work. It was her love and guidance that showed me the way to the light at the end of the tunnel.

Susan Gallagher, who helped me express the essence of these Agreements in the fewest possible words, and who listened to me *ad nauseum* during our many walks in nature about every little detail of this work's unfolding.

My dear friends who read early versions of the manuscript, gave me much valued feedback, and wrote love notes: Judith Bonfoey, Marion Culhane, Ward Flynn, David Neenan, Vivian Saccucci, Laurie Weiss and Sandy Westin.

Nick Gordon, my local brother, who offers insights from a deep well of experience and wisdom, always from the most loving heart and always in perfect timing.

All those who have published the Revolutionary Agreements in early forms and beautifully modeled their use in front of thousands worldwide toward the admirable goal of co-creating a positive future: especially Barbara Marx Hubbard and Carolyn Anderson.

My heartfelt thanks to Marshall Thurber and his staff of

"Money And You," a personal development program responsible for speeding up my own evolution. Marshall's work is the inspiration for the early Geneva Group Agreements, which later evolved into the Revolutionary Agreements.

Gratitude greater than any words could express is given to the many members of my soul family who have traveled in and out of Geneva Group, meeting every month since 1985 to explore the principles behind these Agreements and embody them in every aspect of their lives.

Above and through all else, I thank the Great Spirit, the Source of All Life. For it is God's Hand of Love that guided this writing, as It guides my life.

$\mathcal{B}$IRTH OF THE
REVOLUTIONARY AGREEMENTS

I don't personally trust any revolution where love is not allowed.
—Maya Angelou

Wouldn't it be wonderful if each of us were born with a little instruction manual for living a positive, loving life? "An Inner Guide to a Happy Outer Life." Not dogma, not something wrapped up in a mystery. Just a simple list of Agreements we can make with ourselves for living a life of joy and fulfillment.

What would a life like that look like? Would it mean being surrounded by family and friends who like and love us for who we truly are, all honoring and supporting one another's personal missions in life while joyously pursuing our own? Being true to ourselves by living our highest values in our workplace as well as at home? Making heartfelt and significant contributions to our communities?

Yes; it would look just like that. How do I know this? Because the lack of such a guide provided my husband Glenn and me, along with some wise friends and colleagues, the impetus to create our own.

It was in 1984, while participating in a personal development program, that I had my first glimmer of the tremendous emotional freedom that could be possible from living such a life.[1] Inspired by principles I had learned in this program, Glenn and I co-founded Geneva Group, a forum for like-minded businesspeople to develop, live and teach these principles.[2] We drafted our first version of the Agreements in 1985, then deepened our experience of them by practicing them in all aspects of our lives and exploring their impact on us, our colleagues, friends and families during monthly gatherings which have continued to this day. As the individuals evolved, so have the Agreements.

In the late 1980s, as the Cold War drew to a close, these Agreements became a foundation for my work as Program Coordinator for a revolutionary conference among Soviet and American citizen-leaders.[3] Shortly thereafter, the magic of these Agreements landed me among the world's foremost parliamentarians and spiritual leaders to facilitate their engagement with each other for the benefit of the world.[4]

Glenn and I also took these Agreements to our business clients, where we pioneered leading-edge processes for team-building and organizational development on every scale ranging from tiny mom-'n'-pops to the Fortune 100. During the next decade with our network marketing company, they were adapted and adopted by the top leaders of more than a quarter of a million independent associates as their Leadership Agreements.

In 1991, I placed a copyright on our Agreements in order to protect our right to use them forever, dubbing them "Revolutionary Agreements."

From that moment on, the Agreements have taken on a life of their own, finding their way outside of our sphere of influence to appear in various forms in places unreached directly by us—on the office wall of the president of one of the world's largest corporations, for example, and on the refrigerator door of a global activist who lives in a faraway state.

The Agreements have been published (in various stages of development) in books and policy documents, including: *Blueprint for Presidential Transition*, a document prepared for President Clinton's transition team (1992)[5]; *Rings of Empowerment*, by Carolyn Anderson, Barbara Marx Hubbard and Marian Head (1993)[6]; *What is the Emperor*

Wearing? Truth-Telling in Business Relationships, by Laurie Weiss (1998)[7]; *Love Styles: Re-Engineering Marriage for the New Millennium*, by Brian Brook (2000)[8]; and *The Co-Creator's Handbook: An Experiential Guide for Discovering Your Life's Purpose and Building a Co-Creative Society*, by Carolyn Anderson and Katharine Roske (2001).[9]

These Agreements have helped guide the collaborative efforts of thousands of participants in international conferences, including the 1988 and 1990 Soviet-American Citizens' Summits in Washington, DC and Moscow; the 1995 "Voices of the Earth" eco-spirituality conference in Boulder; and the 2001 "Summit on Spirituality and Sustainability" in Vancouver, B.C.

Most of all, they have continued to grow, evolve and have extraordinary impact on the lives of those who have had the good fortune to have them posted on their walls and written on their hearts.

$\mathcal{T}$HE ONE AGREEMENT

If you were to embrace just one Revolutionary Agreement and practice it with diligence, that alone could transform your life. The truth is, practicing any one of these Agreements will tend to lead, in time, to all the others, because they are all connected. Really, they are all facets of the same One Agreement.

What is that One? It has been called many things by many people; its premise forms the central message at the heart of the seven major world religions.[10] While no single phrase can adequately capture its essence, I might say that the One Agreement is this:

I agree to be my Self.

Why the capital "S" in "my Self"? To give it the Divine quality it deserves. To remind us that we each emanate from a Divine source; that our lives are a gift from our Creator, and that how we live them is a gift to our Creator—and indeed to all creation.

As I set about to simplify and clarify these Agreements for broader use, I began to have glimpses of this underlying unity. The Agreements (which were at one point as many as sixteen) came to number twelve; those twelve then settled into three groups, representing three core principles: *truth, acceptance* and *gratitude,* which in turn are three facets of the One Agreement.

I agree to be my Self:

I agree to be who I am (truth); to accept others for who they are (acceptance); and to appreciate the gift of this moment (gratitude).

In 2001 I read *The Four Agreements* by don Miguel Ruiz.[11] I was immediately struck by the similarities in the wisdom of Ruiz's book and the essence of our Agreements. Even more, I marveled at how different our paths were, yet how similar the truths to which they pointed.

Ruiz's book has since enjoyed phenomenal popularity; in it, the Toltec master describes a remarkably practical path for personal enlightenment, based on the agreements we hold with ourselves. Ruiz walks the reader through unlearning the old, habitual, self-destructive agreements we learn from our up-bringing and replacing them with four positive agreements that affirm our authenticity, integrity and capacity for self-determination. The result, says Ruiz, is to live a life literally of Heaven on Earth.

Unlike Ruiz, I claim no ancient wisdom tradition nor particular spiritual authority. My path to these principles has been through the pragmatic world of business, education, government service and citizen-diplomacy, as well as by grappling with the less lofty daily realities of marriage, parenthood and friendships.

Nevertheless, encountering Ruiz's work only further affirmed the direction our own work was leading. Ultimately, whether Ruiz's *Four Agreements* or these twelve Revolutionary Agreements, they point to One Agreement: *I agree to be my Self.*

I describe the principles behind the Revolutionary Agreements as much as possible through stories—my stories: not extraordinary, just the stuff of everyday life. I have also sought to add perspective, depth and flavor by offering a selection of quotations from others wiser and more eloquent than I following each Agreement.[12] Finally, at the conclusion of each chapter I offer you a way to anchor the corresponding Agreement in your own life today.

As you read, I expect you will find stories and situations from your own life that make these ideas come alive for you;

in fact, I encourage you to do so. You may want to jot notes in the margin or keep a blank journal handy to note these situations as they occur to you, which will make your reading of *Revolutionary Agreements* richer and more real for you.

Some Agreements may seem obvious to you. Some may feel like too much to deal with right now—you may want to skip over those that do and come back to them later. As with Goldilocks and the three bears' beds, some Agreements will feel "just right," giving you valuable insights you can implement in your life right away. Feel free to skip around to those Agreements that beckon to you. And as you put the Agreements into practice, I invite you to share your own stories with us at www.RevolutionaryAgreements.com.

The Agreements are not my invention or creation. My role in introducing them to you is less that of author and more one of steward, for the Agreements have a life of their own. They are not static; they evolve and take on different meanings over time, becoming richer with experience as we grow and develop. They start as guidelines—and end as wisdom.

Some you may already know intimately; others will deepen in significance for you as you explore their meaning in your life. All are timeless. And timely.

*L*IVING A POSITIVE LIFE

These Agreements seem simple. Really, they *are* simple. At the same time, following them is not so simple—and not always easy. In a world where we are bombarded constantly by negative images, words and actions, it takes courage to live a positive life.

Is it worth it?

My friends and business associates often tell me they think I live a "blessed life." While I acknowledge that blessings, luck or "good karma" may play a role, I must attribute much of my good fortune to living by these simple, powerful Agreements.

Like everyone, I juggle work, family, friendships, household, hobbies, finances, and personal and spiritual growth. In each of these areas, I am challenged every day by a complex maze of circumstances and relationships. Yet as I have observed and tried to follow these Agreements, (sometimes more successfully, sometimes less so!), re-examined and re-absorbed them, over the years they have served as a powerful guide on my journey through the complexities of life.

Following these Agreements has allowed me to create a life filled with moments of such love that I can hardly contain my laughter or tears . . . and often don't! I enjoy a life of meaningful friendships, richly fulfilling work, and constantly increasing insights about who I am and how you and I and all of humanity are connected. The Revolutionary Agreements have allowed me to create a life that works.

So yes—it's worth it!

I pray that you will live these Agreements for your own sake—for more loving relationships with your family and friends, for more creative and productive work with your teammates, and for resolving issues within you that may be keeping you from being all that you can be.

My *greatest* hope is that you will not only live and benefit from these Agreements personally, but also be their spokesperson and advocate, becoming a revolutionary leader in co-creating a positive world.

The possibilities for your life are great beyond measure, both for your own fulfillment and for your contribution to the world around you. Whether you are a public figure who touches hundreds of thousands with your actions and words, or a private person who touches just one other person (who then touches another, who touches another), I know that you have the potential, through the expression of living your own life of truth, acceptance and gratitude, to change the world.

Enjoy the journey!

*T*RUTH

I AGREE TO:

Live my mission.
Speak my truth, with compassion.
Look within when I react.
Keep doing what works and change what doesn't.

*A*CCEPTANCE

I AGREE TO:

Listen with my heart.
Respect our differences.
Resolve conflicts directly.
Honor our choices.

*G*RATITUDE

I AGREE TO:

Give and receive thanks.
See the best in myself and others.
Look for blessings in disguise.
Lighten up!

TRUTH

During times of universal deceit,
telling the truth becomes a revolutionary act.
—George Orwell

$\mathcal{T}$RUTH

The trinity that underlies these twelve Agreements is rooted in the idea of truth. By "truth," I do not mean Truth with a capital T, as in *The* Truth.

I mean *your truth*.

Your truth is what is true for you, right now. It may not necessarily be true for me, or at least not entirely so, but that doesn't mean it isn't true for you. What's more, your truth today may be somewhat different from what your truth was a year ago, or a month ago, or even yesterday. This is sometimes hard to accept, which is one reason we often hold onto relationships, jobs and other situations long after they no longer "ring true" for us.

A magnificent synonym for "your truth" is *authenticity*. Thus, the "One Agreement" could read: *I agree to be my authentic Self.* The principle of truth and authenticity rightfully lies at the heart of all twelve Revolutionary Agreements.

AGREEMENT ONE

I agree
to live
my mission.

Cherish your visions. Cherish your ideals. Cherish the music that stirs in your heart, the beauty that forms in your mind, the loveliness that drapes your purest thoughts, for out of them will grow all delightful conditions, all heavenly environment; of these, if you but remain true to them, your world will at last be built.
— James Allen

Have you ever heard yourself say, "Some day, when I have the time (energy, money, emotional strength), I'll . . ."? How would you finish that sentence? For some people, it might be: ". . . I'll take up painting." Or, ". . . go on a cross-country trip . . . read great books just for pleasure . . . take my kids camping . . . study to be an architect . . . move to a location I truly love." Whatever it is, it's something you really want to do.

But when? When you retire? When you have the money? When the kids grow up? When you have some "free time"? For most people, the sad truth is, "some day" never comes.

Now, here's the really good news: if "some day" seems impossibly far off, we always have *today*. Everyone does. In fact, today is the *only* day we have!

What if you could feel fulfilled today, rather than waiting

for tomorrow? In a very real sense, you can. How? By identifying what it is that you love, what is truly important to you, then letting that guide your daily actions.

This Agreement completely frees us from the "some day . . ." trap. It asks us to identify our mission, then live it—right now, *today*. This Agreement asks us to live our truth—to make our everyday choices and activities an expression of our authentic selves.

Does this mean we can have anything we want? No, of course not. But it does mean we can incorporate the *essence* of what we want into our lives in some way, every day, and be that much closer to living the life of our dreams.

When Alice asked the Cheshire Cat which road she should take, he replied, "That depends a good deal on where you want to get to." "I don't care much where—" she began to say, and he cheerfully replied, "Then it doesn't matter which way you go!"

What road are you taking? Where does it lead? Asking and answering this question is the first step in creating a life of great fulfillment, its rewards the fruit not of lofty and far-away goals, but of the actions of everyday life.

What Is My Mission?

Mission is a magnificent word; it can also be very practical and immediate. Your *mission* is simply your answer to the question, "What would I most love to do?"

For some, "mission" is a calling, what you might call a "life purpose." For others, being "on a mission" has to do with accomplishing a specific goal, which may take years to achieve, or months, or days. For some, this Agreement means "connecting into the mission of the organization I've chosen to work with."

Your mission may be any of these, or all of these, or something else entirely. There's no "right way" to define your mission. Our mission is whatever we choose it to be. The only thing that's important is that it is *your* answer to the question, "What would I most love to do?" What you do speaks clearly about who you are.

Much has been written about the importance of identifying our mission. Author Carolyn Myss describes the process as discovering your "sacred contract" in her book of the same name.[13] In *The Co-Creator's Handbook: An Experiential Guide for Discovering Your Life's Purpose*, Carolyn Anderson and Katharine Roske talk about "being attracted to your chosen work."[14] In *What Should I Do With My Life?*, Po Bronson describes his discovery that our true life mission often comes to us not in a blindingly clear epiphany but, as Bronson puts it, "in a whisper."[15] Learning to follow that whisper may be the most important thing we ever do. In *The 7 Habits of Highly Effective People* and again in *First Things First*, Stephen Covey beautifully explains how easily our mission—those things that are most important to us—can be crowded out of our lives if we let the trivia and minutiae of everyday life take precedence.[16,17]

However you choose to explore, examine and define your mission, the critical thing is to do it, then ask yourself this all-important question: "Is this something I am living every day?"

Your mission needn't be something carved in stone. My own mission has changed many times, and it continues to evolve as I do. As I grow older, I find that my personal purpose has become less task-oriented and more focused on how I live in the present. Today, my mission is:

To enjoy life and experience love in every moment.

Here are some examples of mission statements that have guided me over the years. Some are rather lofty (and make me chuckle as I review them now); some were simple, practical and profoundly life-changing:

- To facilitate the alignment of leaders.
- To foster an environment of genuine collaboration in which everyone feels empowered to express their individual and collective potential.
- To raise a child who is able to make wise decisions about his health and safety and who is capable of giving and receiving love.
- To be a supportive, loving partner.
- To liberate myself and all humanity to realize our full potential.
- To make a positive difference in the life of each person I meet.
- To foster a growing network of people who choose to be physically, emotionally, spiritually and financially healthy.

Feel free to use one of these mission statements if it feels right for you, or adapt one of them to fit you better, or create one that speaks from your own heart. And don't get hung up on the word "mission." Simply consider what gives you great joy and fulfillment.

Take some time to wander through your fondest dreams, visions, goals and purpose. Write down the words that come to you.

Please do this before you continue reading. If you feel stuck, you may want to read one of the books referred to on the previous page or get step-by-step help online at either of these web sites: www.truthzone.com/htdocs/planner.html, or www.franklincovey.com/missionbuilder/index.html.

What I Would Most Love To Do

_____

_____

_____

_____

So, I might say my mission in life is:

_____

_____

_____

_____

Living Courageously

Simply *identifying* your mission can have revolutionary results all by itself. Your mission may make itself felt and start working in your life right away.

You may find, once you've really taken the time to sit down and write out a statement of your mission, vision or purpose, that what you've written doesn't jive with your everyday life. You may want to make some changes . . . possibly even big changes.

This can take courage. Indeed, as I mentioned in the introduction, it takes courage to live a positive life—and I encourage you to do it! Both *courage* and *encourage* come from the same root word, *cor*, which means "heart." Having the courage to find and live your mission means following your heart—"putting your heart into it."

Sometimes people discover that the mission of the organization they belong to is not consistent with their personal values; in other words, they may be in the wrong place. If you are unhappy in your workplace, could it be that you are uncomfortable trying to live your company's mission?

As organizational development consultants, my husband Glenn and I would often warn company executives that when we were finished with our team vision and values work, some of their employees (or even the executives themselves) might choose to leave the organization.

We once offered this cautionary observation to the CEO of a company with about 40 employees. She replied that she understood, and that it was all right: she would rather have only those people who were dedicated to her mission. After we had completed our work with her company, several employees did indeed choose to leave. One of these was a woman who said, "I'm going to sell my house, get an RV and write my book." She had discovered that she didn't connect to the mission of the organization with which she was working. She felt she was wasting her life by not living her own mission.

This woman was no longer willing to settle for "some day . . . ." By identifying what she wanted to be doing *today*, she also left the CEO's company in a stronger position, with greater solidarity of purpose among the remaining employees. This woman's brave decision and her commitment to follow Agreement One resulted in a win for her *and* a win for the company.

Putting My Mission to the Test

In 1985, at the age of 34, I identified my first personal mission: *to facilitate the alignment of leaders.* This clarified desire soon proved to play a defining role in an important life decision. Indeed, it turned out to have a major impact on the rest of my life.

Glenn and I had just finished a two-year business consulting contract and I was ready to make my next major work commitment. Just then, two situations came my way. I was offered a well-paying contract with a major company to help develop its computer-user documentation. At the same time, a good friend asked if I would help her complete preparations for a forthcoming Soviet-American Citizens' Summit to be held in Washington, DC.

The first offer promised all the benefits of a great professional contract: it would engage me in work that would use my technical writing skills, would be nearby my home, and would pay me well. If I accepted the second offer instead, I would have to leave my home for three months' of long days on a project that was behind schedule—and for which I would need to raise funds. At the same time, there was also a certain nobility of purpose and historic dimension to this second option, which was attractive to me.

As I wrestled with this decision, Glenn asked me: "Which situation more closely matches your personal mission? Which is more likely to help you *facilitate the alignment of leaders?*" In other words, Glenn held up the yardstick of Agreement One.

It was no contest.

Little did I know where this short-term commitment would lead. During those three months, President Reagan and President Gorbachev met and officially ended the Cold War. Our bringing together former "enemies" launched collaborative efforts that subtly reshaped history. During that auspicious week in 1988 in Washington, DC, relationships between Soviets and Americans were begun that deepened over the course of more than 300 projects, including annual multinational conferences on education; shared computer technology for environmentally-sound practices; a joint study on the treatment of war trauma; projects promoting the new Soviet entrepreneurships, from handcraft businesses to quick-print shops; collaborative films to expose and eliminate stereotypes; peaceful exchanges among military personnel from different nations; telecommunications projects and space education!

And it didn't stop there. I could not have predicted it at the time, but my decision also opened the door to many more years of fulfilling my mission in other situations—situations I likely would never have discovered otherwise.

Because of our work on the Soviet-American Citizens' Summit, our team was invited to help design the first Global Forum of Spiritual and Parliamentary Leaders on Human Survival in Oxford, England, and then the second Global Forum on the Environment in Moscow. These Summits were to bring together some of the greatest minds and hearts of our generation—people who were typically kept apart—to collaborate on the future of our world.

During these events, I had the privilege of working alongside such leaders as Mother Teresa, the Dalai Lama, the Archbishop of Canterbury, Hopi Elder Thomas Banyanca, Iroquois Chief Oren Lyons, the Very Reverend Dean Morton of St. John's Cathedral in New York, then US Senator Al Gore, cabinet members from countries all over the world, and Soviet President Mikhail Gorbachev, who hosted our closing event of the 1990 Global Forum at the Kremlin in Moscow.

Would any of these opportunities have come into my life if I hadn't clearly defined and followed my personal mission? It's highly doubtful. I am an ordinary person who simply took the time to consider what makes me feel really good, wrote this down as a personal mission statement, and then used it to guide my actions.

Your Mission Lives in the Present

The focus of Agreement One is not on accomplishing a specific mission or goal, but rather on the impact our missions have on our everyday lives. In other words, the importance of your mission is not to *achieve* it, but to *live* it; not to *wish for* it, but to *personify* it.

There is a huge distinction between the two—and recognizing that distinction can make all the difference in the world. This happened, in fact, when I first arrived at the site of preparations for the first Soviet-American Citizens' Summit.

The Summit's stated mission was: "To deepen relationships between Soviet and American citizens by creating and collaborating on joint projects serving their nations and the world." When I first walked into that office (just blocks from the Hart Senate Office Building where I'd worked a few years earlier) with only three months left before the event, I was stunned by the contrast between mission and current reality.

Despite having so mighty and life-changing a mission, the Summit's office environment looked like so many others I had encountered. Chaos reigned; tensions were high; communication was strained. All eyes were on the clock as it ticked away, the three-month deadline looming ominously. There was more work to be done than these intelligent, dedicated and caring people could possibly complete in time. Everyone was getting burned out.

When we arrived, we asked everyone to take a breath. Glenn and I took the staff away for a day of remembering— remembering what they had hoped this mission would accomplish, remembering how they had felt when they first began working together for this noble cause. They reconnected to their chosen mission: *To deepen relationships by creating and collaborating on joint projects.*

If the staff were living that mission every day, they would be deepening relationships among *themselves* as they collaborated on creating the forthcoming Summit—and in so doing, would be serving their goal as well. But without a process to illuminate this connection, this powerful mission was lost in the hustle and bustle of daily preparations and relegated to a hope for the future, rather than serving as a guide for today.

Glenn and I introduced the Revolutionary Agreements to the staff. The group modified them to serve the special needs of this extraordinary project. Everyone agreed to take time each morning to gather together and listen as each member of the team read one Agreement aloud. We began by reading the mission of the Summit and re-committing ourselves to live our chosen mission.

Due to the brilliant inspiration and historic efforts of Rama Vernon, Director of the Center for Soviet-American Dialogue, and Barbara Marx Hubbard, the Summit's visionary Program Chairperson, the result was magnificent. Hundreds of projects were born or fostered that February; many achieved a life of their own over the ensuing years. The Summit staff "walked their talk" by living their mission; as a result, they changed the world.

Mission in the Workplace

Think for a moment about your place of work. Do you know your work mission?

Let's suppose you work for a company whose mission includes these words: "to surprise and delight our customers." How would you live this mission every day?

What would you observe in a workplace where *everyone* lived the mission, "to surprise and delight our customers"? Which would you be more likely to hear: "Sorry, that's not my job," or, "Sure, I'll be glad to help!"? Would you expect to see people meeting the minimum required of them, or striving to do their very best? Would you see people plodding dully through their tasks, or would you see the sparkle of creativity flowing? Might you see spontaneous celebrations when the customers *were* surprised and delighted? (And wouldn't that delight *you*?)

In his wonderful book, *The E-Myth Revisited: Why Most Small Businesses Don't Work and What to Do About It*, Michael Gerber describes his experience of staff embodying their mission at a resort hotel where he happened to stay one night.[18]

The hotel's objective was to give their customers a sense that this was a special place, created by special people, doing what they do in the best possible way. How did that manifest? During the brief check-in process, the clerk made a reservation for Gerber in their restaurant. After his meal, he enjoyed a brandy. Returning to his room eager to light a fire in the fireplace on this chilly night, he found the fire already burning, his bed turned down, and in addition to the usual mints, there was another glass of brandy by his bedside. A card welcomed him for his first stay and invited him to call day or night with any needs. In the morning, he awoke to the smell of coffee and discovered another note: "Your brand of coffee. Enjoy!" A polite knock on the door led him to discover a newspaper. But not just any newspaper—*his favorite* newspaper!

These actions and others like them not only surprised and

delighted Gerber—they also turned him into a customer for life. The employees at that hotel knew the hotel's mission, and they lived it.

What if you and your work team were to spend a few hours together in a relaxed setting to explore the question, "How could we live our mission today?" How might this approach enhance your work life? And how might this strategy positively affect the people who are the beneficiaries of your organization's mission?

Mission in the Schools

What would happen if the people who ran our schools and classrooms were guided by an official mission? My son's elementary school, Eagle Crest, had such a mission, fashioned around an anagram for "Eagle":

> **E**xpect nothing less than success!
> **A**lways think before we act.
> **G**row and learn in new and different ways.
> **L**earn to accept responsibility for our actions.
> **E**veryone practices kindness and consideration.

What if our schools' staff members—principals, teachers, administrative staff, janitors—lived such a mission as a model for our children and our communities? If school administrators were to truly "expect nothing less than success," they would hold their teachers and our children in the highest esteem, expecting all of them to reach the height of their potential.

What if practicing "kindness and consideration" were regularly noticed and rewarded? How might this affect the choices our children make? Indeed, Michael's school *did* practice this. As a result, the children were often rewarded by the principal when caught doing something that exceeded their daily pledge of this mission statement. In other words, as Kenneth Blanchard and Spencer Johnson put it in their classic *The One-Minute Manager*, they were routinely "caught doing something right."[19]

Mission in the Family

What kind of impact would it have if you and your family created a *family mission*? What would you like to accomplish together? What kind of interactions would you like to have?

What if once a week, or once a month (or even once a year!) you sat down together to review your mission statement and consider how well you were all doing in living your family's mission?

Regardless of our backgrounds, we share one thing in common: at the core of our being is a desire to love and be loved. What if each of us consciously chose to include "loving" as a part of our individual mission? And what if we let this mission guide our daily actions? Surely our lives would never be the same. Indeed, we would have changed our world in the blink of an eye.

On the next page is a mission statement that Glenn and I and our son Michael co-created for our family. After we had finished writing it, we laminated it and now display it prominently in our home.

"I agree to live my mission" is the first of these twelve pathways for living a positive life. Take the time to consider how to embody this agreement so that rather than working *towards* fulfilling your mission, your mission gives you the fulfillment you deserve *today*.

TO LOVE AND RESPECT
- A 15 YEAR PACT -

We, Michael Justin Head, Marian Linda Head and Glenn Eugene Head, enter into this agreement on July 4, 1999 with gladness and joy. We choose to treat each other with respect, honoring each other as the unique individuals we are. Although there are times when we may disagree, we will refrain from being nasty and mean, endeavoring to always be loving and respectful.

We understand that there may be times that we forget this agreement, and we ask of each other that we be gently reminded, and allowed 24 hours to fully remember and begin once again to treat each other with respect. We will always forgive each other these short lapses, and remember that we are family, forever bonded in love through God our Creator.

By signing below, we show our agreement to treat each other with love and respect for 15 years, at which time this agreement is renewable.

| Michael Justin Head | Marian Linda Head | Glenn Eugene Head |

Words of Wisdom
"I agree to live my mission."

Destiny is no matter of chance; it is a matter of choice.
It is not a thing to be waited for; it is a thing to be achieved.
—William Jennings Bryan

Man's ideal state is realized when he has fulfilled the purpose for which
he is born. And what is it that reason demands of him? Something
very easy—that he live in accordance with his own nature.
—Seneca

When you are making a success of something,
it's not work. It's a way of life.
—Andrew Granatelli

I dream my painting,
and then I paint my dream.
—Vincent Van Gogh

It's not enough to have lived.
We should be determined to live for something.
May I suggest that it be creating joy for others,
sharing what we have for the betterment of personkind,
bringing hope to the lost and love to the lonely.
—Leo Buscaglia

First say to yourself what you would be;
and then do what you have to do.
—Epictetus

How wonderful it is that nobody need wait a single moment
before starting to improve the world.
—Anne Frank

All know the way;
few actually walk it.
—Bodhidharma

The single most important thing
you can do in business is to be yourself.
—Sherry Lansing

Concentrate all your thoughts on the task at hand.
The sun's rays do not burn until brought to a focus.
—Alexander Graham Bell

Here is a test to find whether
your mission on earth is finished:
If you're alive, it isn't.
—Richard Bach

When you discover your mission, you will feel its demand.
It will fill you with enthusiasm
and a burning desire to get to work on it.
—W. Clement Stone

Don't ask yourself what the world needs; ask yourself
what makes you come alive. And then go do that.
—Harold Whitman

To believe in something, and not to live it, is dishonest.
—Mahatma Gandhi

Focus on Today
I agree to live my mission—TODAY!

Here are a few simple steps you can take to more fully live the truth of who you are, today and every day. Write your answers in your journal—then follow your heart's desire!

1. My mission (passion, purpose, vision, or dream) is to:
   Example: Have the financial freedom to follow my heart every day.

2. What are three ways I can experience the essence of my mission every day?
   Example: Make walking with a different friend every day a priority. This is following my heart and also helps my pursuit of financial freedom: my friends are wise counselors and advisors, and we inspire each other.

3. What is one small change I can make *today* to live the essence of my mission?
   Example: Enjoy fun, relaxing time after dinner each evening playing with my family, rather than returning to my home office to work.

AGREEMENT TWO

I agree to speak my truth, with compassion.

A truth that disheartens because it is true
is of more value than the most stimulating of falsehoods.
—Maurice Maeterlinck

While the first Agreement focuses on our actions, the second focuses on our words. The two go hand in hand; authenticity in both deed and word is the manifestation of being true to your Self.

The phrase "my truth" is important here: again, "my truth" is not necessarily "*the* Truth." It is what is true *for me*—my personal opinion, perspective, and belief. When we understand that truth is relative, we are freed to speak our own truth without malice, judgment or the piercing arrows of "I'm right; you're wrong."

...With Compassion

Why "with compassion"? Because the decision to live and speak our truth does not give us license to go about dumping whatever's on our minds. "With compassion" means having sensitivity to the people around us. We have our truth; others have theirs, too. We are not the center of the universe.

Speaking your truth also has to do with how other people receive that truth. You speak, and at the same time also feel the other person's perspective. Imagine an infinity symbol passing in the air between you and me. True communication makes a complete loop between the two of us; "speaking our truth" can never be a one-way process.

What We Fear

Why doesn't everyone speak his or her truth? For me, the reason was fear of rejection.

My long-time need to feel accepted challenged my ability to follow this Agreement. My word became my armor rather than a portal to my inner light. Armor can have the opposite effect from its intention: rather than protecting us, it keeps us separated from the close, fulfilling relationships we desire.

Instead of drawing people to the light that emanates from us when we're feeling self-love and self-acceptance, our self-protective falsehoods tend to repel those sensitive enough to feel that something "isn't quite right" with our communication.

Another reason some of us button up rather than speak our truth is the fear of creating animosity, our desire to maintain harmony at all costs. My father was adamant that, "Nothing's worth fighting about. It's more important to keep the peace." This certainly had an impact on the way I handled conflict—or more accurately, how I didn't.

In my first marriage, I spent many years acting as though everything were just fine, when in fact, I felt an inner pain burning constantly. Everything was not at all "just fine," but I hadn't the courage to say so.

One day, in a therapy session designed to help my husband and me speak our truths to each other, I surprised both of us by blurting out, "I feel like a fake! My whole life feels like a fake!" I had spent years lying about my feelings not only to my husband, but to myself as well. (The ulcers and migraines should have been a clue!)

When I later learned to practice this Agreement in its fullness, the reward was a peacefulness in my heart and my soul that I had not experienced before. Recognizing and speaking my truth brought with it a sense of being in full integrity. It was not easy to break old habits, but it was worth it.

Little White Lies

Many of us have come to accept living with lies as normal, especially "little white lies." Telling little white lies is a seductive thing. We do this ostensibly to avoid hurting other people's feelings or to avoid some other sort of conflict, so the practice can appear to have noble motivation.

Yet it is a profoundly destructive habit. Why so? Because it undermines trust. When people hear you speak little white lies, they learn not to take what you say at face value. It's like building a house on sand: there's no foundation.

Years ago, my mom had a pattern of creating stories to support her actions in which I would be the bad guy and she would be the angel. It was so subtle, I don't think she was even aware of it. "I don't want to stay at your home for longer than four nights," she might say. "I don't want to be in your way. You're too busy to have company for longer than that."

An uneasy feeling would set in. Where did this "four nights" idea come from? Did I actually say I was too busy? I didn't think so. What was she getting at? Sometimes her statement became round one of a game. My next move would be to show her how much I cared for her by trying to convince her to change her mind and stay longer. It was frustrating: I was being blamed for her decision, and I knew darn well she wasn't being completely honest with me.

Finally I asked her outright: "Do you mean you don't want to stay longer than four nights, because by then you'll be ready to get home to your friends and your routine? Or do you mean that you don't like it when I don't make time for you when you come to visit?"

The truth was, she meant both of those things at different times, and neither one was easy for her to admit.

Eventually we got this all out on the table, and she agreed to be honest with me. Now she will tell me how much she loves being with me and my family (which is true) and how difficult it is for her to miss too many of her activities with her friends (which is also true). And, she might ask me when would be the best time for her to visit so that we would be least interrupted by the work I love (which shows compassion for me).

The power of the truth is always greater than the reason for the lie.

Even a six-year old is wise enough to know the difference between the truth and "little white lies."

Glenn and I were touring an assisted living center once with Glenn's mom; our little son Michael was with us. As we walked through one room, Michael spied an enormous jar filled with cookies and asked, "May I have one?" We said, "of course." He finished his cookie, then asked if he might go back and get another—to which Nana replied, "No." When Michael started to fuss, she said, "They're all gone." Perplexed by this confusing response, Michael didn't know what to do but pout.

Do we endear ourselves to our children (and grandchildren) by avoiding conflicts with obvious falsehood...or do we instead earn their distrust?

How do you feel when someone says something to you that doesn't ring true? "We're sorry we can't come to dinner; Suzie has a headache." The speaker may think this is an easy way out that hurts no one. But how much greater trust and deeper friendship would result if he were to say instead, "Thanks so much for inviting us; tonight's not going to work for us. We've been looking forward to a night out alone, and this is the night we'd picked."

A friendship built upon lies—even those "harmless little white" ones—is a house of cards; sooner or later it will fall.

The Power of Telling the Truth

Can you imagine how it would feel to know you could ask your friends for anything, and they would always tell you the truth in response? Perhaps you have friendships where this is true. If so, then you already know it is one of the most wonderful feelings there is!

One of my best friends, Peggy, is a great model for living this agreement.

"Would you like to come for dinner tonight?" I will ask her.

"No," answers Peggy; "I'm really needing family time tonight. Let's do it another time."

No headaches, no excuses. Just the truth. How refreshing!

In addition to establishing a foundation of trust in our friendships, speaking our truth is the most direct path to reestablishing harmony when it has been disrupted or conflict has arisen.

"I feel disconnected from you." Or,
"Something doesn't feel right. What just happened?"

No blame, just a desire to reconnect. Truth maintains an inner integrity that links to integrity in others, forming the angles of the sacred geometry of our relationships. Without integrity, there is no true connection. With truth, relationships can become extraordinary.

Politeness at the Expense of Honesty

When I ask a friend for a favor, I expect her to respond by letting me know honestly whether or not she has both the ability and desire to fulfill it. Unfortunately, many people are raised to be polite to others (a good thing) at the expense of honesty (not such a good thing). This created a major rift once with a good friend, "Linda."

Occasionally I would ask her, "Would you mind if our son stayed at your home for an hour after school, and we'll pick him up later?"

One time, Linda replied, "Sure, I'd love that…but I don't know, I've got to get to the store today to pick up some things." To which I jumped in helpfully, "I'll be going by that store this morning. I'd be happy to pick up what you need!"

I thought I was being helpful. To Linda, this felt manipulative: I should have picked up her hint and withdrawn my request! Since she didn't say a word about it to me, I would never have known her perspective…if she hadn't complained to a mutual friend that I was "using her." When the friend shared this with me, I was shocked. I had no idea that my request had been an imposition! I thought angrily, "Why didn't she tell *me*?" I made a date to get together with Linda to see if we could relieve the mounting tension between us.

I was nervous about the meeting. Our friendship was important to me. I was angry at her behind-my-back talk, confused about why she wouldn't just tell me what was on her mind in the first place, and afraid of the repercussions of this conflict. It turned out to be an enlightening encounter for both of us.

"When someone asks me a favor," Linda explained, "I was taught to always say 'yes.'" Thus, she often felt stuck doing things she didn't want to do. Linda and I placed different values on truth-telling and neighborliness.

We agreed that if Linda had simply said, "It doesn't really work for me to do that today," delivering the message cleanly and without guilt, I would have received and appreciated her honesty. No justification needed; just the simple truth.

After that incident, I said to Glenn, "I'd rather have one or two friends who tell me the truth than a hundred friends who choose politeness over honesty!"

A World of Truth

Can you see how readily this Revolutionary Agreement could transform the workplace? Imagine what life would be like if your teammates, employees, supervisors and peers all told you their truth—with compassion?

I learned from Barbara Marx Hubbard to think of each of my work teams as an astronaut corps.

If I were an astronaut, would I withhold my truth about my teammates' performance? No way! If we depended on each other for our very lives, you'd better believe we'd be telling each other the truth—with or without compassion! (And here's a striking thought: we *do* depend on each other for our very lives!)

Astronaut corps are comprised of people with diverse backgrounds and experience. The crew of the space shuttle Columbia included men and women who were Hindu, Roman Catholic, Jewish, Charismatic Christian, Unitarian, Episcopalian and Baptist by faith. By heritage they were Indian, Israeli, American; by race, black, white and brown. Each brought unique perspectives (personal truths), yet each was committed to the highest level of personal excellence and teamwork towards the accomplishment of their joint mission.[20]

The diversity of our teams is what gives us the greatest possibilities for creativity, innovation, synergy, and excellence beyond bounds. When teammates learn to speak their truth, with compassion, the possibilities for personal and collective success become limitless.

Telling the Truth to Our Customers

Truthful relationships with our customers is vital. One of the challenges I faced at first with my career as a network marketer was overcoming the image of sales as a profession that depended on manipulating the truth. (My mother reveals this common bias, for example, when she introduces me to others by explaining what I do—then adding, with an obvious mix of delight, pride and incredulity, "And she always tells the truth!")

I have been told by my associates and customers that my success in the networking profession is due in large part to my authenticity and the straightforward and honest way I present my products and opportunity. I continue to be amazed and saddened by all those businesspeople who feel they must exaggerate the truth in order to achieve success, even when their products and services would stand perfectly well enough on their own merits.

Consider relationships you have as a customer of others. Are the enduring ones built upon a strong foundation of trust? And is that trust based upon honest communications? If so, then wouldn't you want to offer the same to your own customers? There is no more important ingredient in a successful businessperson's life than the powerful force of relationships based on honesty and integrity.

Telling the Truth in Politics

Many of us living in the United States learned in elementary school that George Washington said, "I cannot tell a lie: I cut down the cherry tree." Unfortunately, for most of us, our impression of honesty in government has gone downhill ever since!

For most of my lifetime, I have seen our society struggle to deal with dishonesty at all levels of government. Yet who is the "government"? In the United States, it is "for the people, by the people and of the people." With all the talk of political reform, with the citizenry vacillating between outrage and resignation, what are we to do?

We certainly need a revolution—*now*! And that revolution can only come from within. The change we need is not simply one within the political process, but one within ourselves. "The fault, dear Brutus," says Cassius in Shakespeare's *Julius Caesar*, "lies not in our stars but in ourselves." And so does the solution. We will enjoy greater honesty in government when we embody it.

Join the thousands of us who are leading this movement to live positive lives. Become a leader in your workplace, your home, and your community. Learn to speak your truth, with compassion for others and yourself, and you will experience greater peace, wellness and abundance. Your integrity will serve as an example for others, forming the foundation for lasting friendships, productive work teams and communities that truly serve the people.

Words of Wisdom
"I agree to speak my truth, with compassion."

Truth and tears clear the way
to a deep and lasting friendship.
—Marie de Sevigne

Level with your child by being honest.
Nobody spots a phony quicker than a child.
—Mary MacCracken

Where is there dignity
unless there is honesty?
—Marcus Tullius Cicero

When in doubt, tell the truth.
—Mark Twain

Our lives improve only when we take chances—
and the first and most difficult risk we can take
is to be honest with ourselves.
—Walter Anderson

If it is not seemly, do it not;
if it is not true, speak it not.
—Marcus Aurelius Antoninus

He's true to God who's true to man.
—James Russell Lowell

Love truth, but pardon error.
—Voltaire

I hope I shall possess firmness and virtue enough
to maintain what I consider the most enviable of all titles,
the character of an honest man.
—George Washington

I love you, and because I love you,
I would sooner have you hate me for telling you the truth
than adore me for telling you lies.
—Pietro Aretino

Those who think it's permissible to tell white lies
soon grown color-blind.
—Austin O'Malley

A lie will easily get you out of a scrape, and yet,
strangely and beautifully, rapture possesses you
when you have taken the scrape and left out the lie.
—Charles Edward Montague

Never apologize for showing feeling. When you do so,
you apologize for the truth.
—Benjamin Disraeli

Speaking from the heart frees us from the secrets that burden us.
—Sara Paddison

I believe that unarmed truth and unconditional love
will have the final word in reality.
—Martin Luther King, Jr.

Focus on Today
I agree to speak my truth, with compassion—TODAY!

Here are a few simple steps you can take to enhance your awareness and practice speaking your truth, with compassion. Record your thoughts in your journal.

1. Choosing three family members and/or friends I interact with most, honestly answer these two questions for each:

    Do I *always* speak my truth with this person?

    Do I *always* speak with compassion, considering this person's feelings?

2. If the answer was "no" to either question above, then:

    Am I willing to practice speaking my truth, with compassion, with this person at least once each day we're together?

    When or in what situation will I initiate compassionate truth-telling with this person? On what topic?

3. Choosing three people from work I interact with most, honestly answer these two questions for each:

    Do I *always* speak my truth with this person?

    Do I *always* speak with compassion, considering this person's feelings?

4. If the answer was "no" to either question above, then:

    Am I willing to practice speaking my truth, with compassion, with this person at least once each day we're together?

    When or in what situation will I initiate compassionate truth-telling with this person? On what topic?

AGREEMENT THREE

I agree
to look within
when I react.

It is only imperfection that complains of what is imperfect.
The more perfect we are the more gentle and
quiet we become towards the defects of others.
—Joseph Addison

That person is so mean . . ." "She is so manipulative . . ." "He is so prejudiced . . ."

It's one thing to observe someone behaving or speaking negatively; it's another altogether to be *consumed* by our negative feelings about that person or behavior. I've learned (the hard way) that when someone's actions cause us emotional distress, we have an opportunity for healing—specifically, for healing *ourselves*.

How I Learned This Agreement

My mother-in-law was visiting us in Colorado. During one evening together, she said so many things I perceived as mean, manipulative and hurtful that I found myself in a complete frenzy.

I had *never* been spoken to that way! How *could* she! I couldn't stay in my house with her *one moment longer*! What was I to *do*? I frantically searched for a reason to leave for a few days. She was *horrible*! I felt as though I *hated* her!

—and this was especially painful to hear myself saying. From the time I was young, I always strove to integrate my father's advice into my life: "Life is too short to hate anyone." *Hate* was an out-of-control, angry, loaded, despicable word I had projected onto another person only one other time in my entire life.

I knew I was in trouble, and had nowhere to turn. I prayed …and my prayer was answered.

Ahden, a dear friend and psychologist who was staying with us at the time, said, "Marian, if you are willing to take a deep, hard look at *yourself*, I can help you."

"What do you mean?" I asked, perplexed and still angry. My friend then revealed the message behind this Agreement.

"When you have such a powerful emotional reaction to what someone else says, it usually has to do with a part of yourself that you don't like."

This was difficult for me to accept. What could she possibly be talking about? I was a *nice* person. I wasn't mean and manipulative. Ahden was patient with me.

"Has there ever been a time when you feel you were manipulative?" I searched inside myself and had to admit that, yes, there had been such a time. "And how do you feel about that part of yourself?" she asked. Not good, I admitted; uncomfortable; embarrassed; bad. Hmmm.

"How about mean? Have you ever been mean to someone?" she asked. I considered this, and had to admit that I hadn't always been sugar, spice and everything nice to my own mother. And how did I feel about that? Well, it didn't make me feel like an angel.

Strangely enough, as I began to uncover my hidden self-judgment, rather than feeling worse, I actually began to relax.

The anger I felt toward my mother-in-law was dissipating.

"So what do I do about it?" I asked.

"You've already taken a huge step," she explained. "Just being *aware* that these strong feelings which you thought were about your mother-in-law's behavior are really about *yourself* should diffuse your anguish about her. What you choose to do about those feelings themselves is really up to you." I nodded.

"You can learn to embrace all parts of yourself," she continued, "knowing that you make the best choice or decision in every moment, given your current circumstances and wisdom. You can change those things about yourself that you don't like. Or you can leave those parts alone, knowing that you just don't like it when you behave that way. It's up to you."

It was a miracle. The next day, I saw my mother-in-law in a completely new light. It wasn't about *her* anymore. The fire burning beneath my explosive emotion had been put out by this new insight. I no longer held her accountable for my feelings.

It simply changed my life.

Shortly after this episode, we added this important Agreement to our Geneva Group list of Agreements. To this day, I continue to be amazed at how the power of this wisdom can blow apart my strongest negative emotions directed at other human beings. Practicing this Agreement has transformed my reactions from anger to compassion, from hate to love.

We Control Our Own Buttons

Practicing this Agreement has also taught me that no one can *make* me feel a certain way.

In 1984, when my mother-in-law was visiting me in Washington DC, she referred to a group of God's children by a name I felt was derogatory. I was incensed; her remarks cut into me and bothered me deeply for a long time.

Years later, when she visited us in Colorado, I noticed something fascinating: she continued to speak in the same way, using this same language—only now I was simply *noticing* it. I didn't care for the racial slur any more now than I had then … but I was no longer having that same emotional response.

What was the difference? Back in 1984, *I was still grappling with my own prejudices.* They weren't the same as hers, but prejudice is prejudice. Now, many years and experiences later, I had shed much of my own ignorance and cut the cords of intolerance that had bound me so strongly to those words of hers that had pushed my buttons.

When someone says, "He really knows how to push my buttons," just what are those "buttons" anyway, and exactly what are they connected to? I've noticed that my "buttons" are connected to the feelings I have about myself, unresolved feelings that create a great weight which I carry around with me—until I accept myself unconditionally.

I still didn't care for the terms my mother-in-law was using. It's just that her using them no longer pushed my buttons.

I have also learned that most things I say to others with a strong emotional charge turn out, upon examination, to be about myself. What I like in others, I tend to like in myself. What I don't like in others is exactly that which I do not like in myself … even when that's hard to admit.

This is not an easy Agreement for me to keep. It is much easier to blame someone else for how I feel than to take the time and energy to look within and accept full responsibility for my feelings. Yet how we *feel* is surely one of those precious few areas of our lives over which we *can* claim full control. Our feelings are our own. Someone can strike out at us and even damage us physically, but no one can grab hold of our feelings and squeeze the life out of them. Only we have the power to allow or disallow this.

It's Not Personal

When I hear someone make a comment or pass a judgment about me, I now consider that it may be in some way related to that person's concept of him- or herself. For the most part, I believe we judge others based on what is in our minds and on our hearts *about ourselves*, and not about the person we are speaking to or about.

Knowing this has turned my life upside down. I used to take people's critical comments to heart, particularly when they were spoken with great emotion by someone close to me. That was because I thought it was actually about me. No more!

When I first read don Miguel Ruiz's book *The Four Agreements*, I was intrigued and gratified to notice that his Second Agreement is, "Don't take anything personally."[21] He is absolutely right—because it's *not* personal.

Can you see how embracing this Agreement could change your life? In this very moment? To *know* that each of us has our "buttons," and that we often push another's when we are dealing with our own stuff? Can you imagine the compassion we would have for each other if everyone were aware of this? Or the compassion you can have for yourself, and for those with whom you are in relationship, starting right now?

It's worth the pain and effort to search for those unresolved issues within us that trigger strong reactions to what others say or do. The result is wisdom, compassion and love—for others and for oneself.

Words of Wisdom
"I agree to look within when I react."

When you see a man of worth,
think how to rise to his level.
When you see an unworthy man,
then look within and examine yourself.
—Confucius

Know thyself.
—Inscription on the Delphic Oracle[22]

O, happy the soul that saw its own faults.
—Mevlana Rumi

No man can produce great things
who is not thoroughly sincere in dealing with himself.
—James Russell Lowell

Turbulence is life force. It is opportunity.
Let's love turbulence and use it for change.
—Ramsay Clark

Let the refining and improving of your own life
keep you so busy that you have
little time to criticize others.
—H. Jackson Brown, Jr.

The unexamined life is not worth living.
—Socrates

Everything that irritates us about others
can lead us to an understanding of ourselves
—Carl Jung

A lively, disinterested, persistent looking for truth
is extraordinarily rare. Action and faith enslave thought,
both of them in order not to be troubled or inconvenienced
by reflection, criticism or doubt.
—Henri Frédéric Amiel

Everyone thinks of changing the world,
but no one thinks of changing himself.
—Leo Tolstoy

Only by much searching and mining
are gold and diamonds obtained
and man can find every truth connected with his being
if he will dig deep into the mine of his soul.
—James Allen

If you cannot tell the truth about yourself
you cannot tell it about other people.
—Virginia Woolf

People travel to wonder at the height of the mountains,
at the huge waves of the seas, at the long course of the rivers,
at the vast compass of the ocean, at the circular motion of the
stars, and yet they pass by themselves without wondering.
—St. Augustine

Focus on Today
I agree to look within when I react—TODAY!

Here are a few simple steps you can take to reduce stressful reactions you have to the way others behave, while getting to know yourself even better. Record your thoughts in your journal.

1. Some people really annoy me or make me angry. Here are three I can think of who have a tendency to trigger strong emotions in me when they behave in certain ways.
   Example: HW speaks badly about others behind their backs

2. Now it's time to go "soul searching." For each of the behaviors I listed, I'm going to dig deep until I find something in my own behavior (even if it's from ages ago) that is similar. This may be uncomfortable, but it'll be worth it!
   Example: I complained to LZ about how HW does that!

3. The final step is to ask myself, "How do I feel when I behave that way?" or, "How do I feel about my behaving that way in the past?"
   Example: I felt vindictive and nasty for talking behind HIS back!

4. The next time I notice someone exhibiting this same behavior, I will ask myself, "Is my strong emotional reaction tempered now, or even gone altogether?" I'll do my best to remember that it's the way I feel about my *own* behavior that often triggers my disproportionate reaction to similar behaviors in others. It's as though that person holds up a mirror for me to see what I don't like about myself. What I choose to do about my own behavior is not the issue here; it's to disengage from blaming someone else for the way I feel about myself! I will record these incidents that no longer "push my buttons."

AGREEMENT FOUR

I agree to keep doing what works and change what doesn't.

Insanity is doing the same thing over and over again and expecting different results.
—Albert Einstein

Do you ever feel imprisoned by your circumstances, wishing you were somewhere else, with someone else, doing something else? What if, instead of feeling stuck, you could set yourself free?

Glenn used to feel frustrated because he was giving up time he could have spent in other pursuits to drive our son Michael to the gym four times a week. He was faced with a choice.

1) He could continue driving Michael to the gym and feel victimized by having to do it.

2) He could stop driving Michael to the gym.

3) He could change his attitude about driving Michael to the gym and, instead of seeing it as an interruption in his life, look forward to time alone with his son in the car. He could also choose to feel good about contributing to all the benefits

our son derived from his gym practice—a healthy, strong, flexible body; admirable friends; practice at goal-setting and achieving; building self-esteem and self-confidence; and so much more.

He chose option #3.

When first faced with his frustration at this task, he could have said, "I don't *choose* to drive him, I *have* to drive him!" If he had framed it that way, he likely wouldn't have seen all the possibilities and rewards available in the situation. But he didn't; he framed it as a *choice*. Why? Because he chooses to feel free rather than imprisoned by his actions and attitudes. He understands and lives this Agreement.

This fourth Revolutionary Agreement encourages us to stop whining and start winning; to dig ourselves out of holes into which we've either fallen or dug ourselves deeply; to stop complaining, justifying or blaming others for our condition in life, and to choose a new path that may work better for all involved.

In the brilliant little book, *Who Moved My Cheese?*, two tiny human characters, Hem and Haw, feel stuck and powerless.[23] They show up every day at the same place in their maze, expecting to find the cheese that had been there day after day. When the cheese no longer appears, they are at a loss. They don't know how to change old habits; they know only how to continue doing what no longer works.

On the other hand, the two mice in the story, Sniff and Scurry, adapt immediately to the change and move on to find the cheese in a different part of the maze. No stress, no struggle. They are simple creatures, unburdened by analysis paralysis and human expectations. The cheese had moved, and so must they. They know Agreement Four instinctively!

Choose and Re-choose

People often remain in situations that have long ceased to be productive and have instead become an ongoing struggle.

I married young and stayed in my first marriage for eleven years, long after it had stopped working for either of us. If we'd had the habit of honestly reexamining what was and wasn't working, we may have ended our marriage many years earlier—and it would have given us both a new start on life that much sooner.

Having learned what doesn't work, Glenn and I choose to honor and celebrate every precious moment in our lives, rather than committing to a future that is truly unknown. Our 1984 wedding vows reflected this: *"Marriage is not the day of commitment, but the acknowledgement of it; It is not a vow to be, but a recognition of what is; It is not for forever, it is for infinite todays."*

Our friends Lu and Ron celebrated their thirtieth wedding anniversary with a rededication ceremony, where they said their marriage vows and "got married all over again" as a way of reaffirming their choice. What a lovely idea!

What would our lives be like if we reaffirmed our choices daily? We can—and this doesn't apply only to the bigger choices in our lives, like marriage and career; it applies equally to the "little things in life." And sometimes they are not really so little: it is often those simple, daily choices we make that create the life we truly desire—especially the choice of how we spend our time and with whom we spend it.

We are all capable of choosing and re-choosing. Notice the difference between saying, "I *have* to go to work today," and, "I *choose* to go to work today." Do you choose it? You did at one time. What is the effect today of that choice? Does it still serve you? Are you choosing to keep doing what works? Or is it time to change what no longer works in your life?

Allow yourself to choose, notice the effects of your choices, and then re-choose based on your experience. "I choose to volunteer for this program." "I choose to work with this company." "I choose and re-choose this marriage." Only with the freedom to choose do we give ourselves wholly and completely to that which we choose.

An Ideal Situation

For about eight years, Glenn and I participated in developing a cohousing community in Colorado.

Cohousing is a brilliant approach to re-creating the best ideals of the villages of yesteryear, when neighbors knew and cared about each other's well being. Seeded in Denmark decades ago, this type of community-created neighborhood caught on in the US in a huge way in the 1980s, resulting in the development of more than 100 successful cohousing communities throughout North America today.[24]

The arrangement offered us tremendous opportunities to choose (and re-choose) among different areas of contribution. From locating the cohousing site to developing the land, drafting covenants, doing legal and financial work, designing processes for communication and conflict resolution, creating community activities, designing the community center, and more, there was plenty to choose from.

Since we had committed as a community to living our mission—"To support one another in achieving our life purposes"—we allowed each other the freedom to choose whatever tasks supported each of us in giving our best. When anyone created a void by opting out of a given task force, someone else with a new level of energy and commitment often filled that void. This never failed to surprise and delight me.

It felt like an "ideal situation." And indeed it was—for a time. But things change.

After eight years of focused effort on creating our own community, giving a huge amount of our time and energy, we ultimately re-chose: we decided not to continue and to move to a home elsewhere.

It was a difficult decision and felt at first as confusing and painful as a divorce. Ultimately, moving into an already-established neighborhood in a geographical area more conducive to our growing son's activities proved to better serve our family's needs. And because our cohousing community lived by the Geneva Group Agreements, foundational to the Revolutionary Agreements, our friends supported us in changing what was no longer working for us. We suffered none of the wrath that typically erupts when someone on a team has a change of heart or mind.

Freedom to Change at Work

Imagine this type of support in the workplace. With good communication, ample trust and common goals, people can feel free to speak up to change what's not working, and thus serve their businesses' missions at the highest level.

When working with our corporate clients, Glenn and I would sometimes institute weekly half-hour check-ins with each team. First, team members were given "bragging rights," an uplifting way to kick off the check-in by celebrating what *was* working. Each team member then had an opportunity to speak to something that was *not* working. These items were captured on the left side of a flip chart under the heading "What" and next to two blank columns headed "Who" and "When."

When all team members had had an opportunity to speak about what was not working that needed their attention, the facilitator would return to the top item and team members would then assign themselves to the items of greatest interest to them. The resulting self-selected teams would each choose a date to implement the change or to meet and determine a strategy for implementing that change.

This highly efficient process cleared out problems before they had time to fester, put the solutions in the hands of those most affected by the problems, and gave team members an opportunity to champion changes that resulted in benefits for themselves, their teams and their organizations.

Examining My Day

This agreement is as important for mundane, everyday actions as it is for the greater aspects of our lives; all the little frustrations caused by what's not working can so easily add up to stifle our creativity, productivity and contribution in the world.

There was a time when mornings didn't work well for me. This is the time of day when I'm at my best, and every aspect of my being seemed to vie for my attention. *Snuggle in with my husband. Strengthen and condition my body. Meditate. Respond to e-mail. Plan my workday. Fix Michael breakfast and help him get ready for school.*

The tension was enormous. Irritability was high. (That's a sure sign to notice it may be time to change what isn't working.)

I tried different combinations: Setting my alarm to get up earlier. Pleading with Michael not to disturb me until I'd finished having my quiet time. Making his lunch the night before.

Each had its drawbacks: Sandwiches made the night before were soggy, then uneaten at lunchtime. Waking to an early alarm left me feeling tired and grumpy. And my quiet time to feel connected to God was often shattered by a well-meaning child who wanted to feel connected with his mother!

Ultimately, I discovered what worked. I let myself wake up when I woke up, naturally. If it were God's plan for me to meditate or write, I would awaken early enough to do so. Whatever I was doing and however long I'd had to do it, at 7:00 A.M. I wrapped it up to join Michael for the next hour. Instead of feeling trapped by having to get everything done, I was relaxed and happy to have this special hour together. With plenty of time to make his breakfast, prepare a nutritious lunch, test his spelling acuity, and have meaningful discussions, I felt truly blessed to be his parent, rather than annoyed and frazzled!

This small but significant change helped me start my days

feeling more relaxed and joyful. It was well worth the time and care it took to identify what was and wasn't working for me and then take action to make the changes I needed.

When a situation begins to no longer work, we tend to let it build up and become a drama—the drama of the hopeless situation. Once we reach the point where we know something isn't working, it makes so much more sense to stop, identify it and take steps to change it, by changing either what we do or how we feel about it.

Notice in your own life: Where is there drama? Ask yourself, "Is there something that isn't working here? What would happen if I changed what isn't working?" If you like the answer, then you might ask yourself, "Well, what am I waiting for?!" (Does waiting work for you?)

Consider making a list of ten things that are working for you and ten things that are not. Listing those things that *are* working for you is just as important as listing those that aren't, so that when you start eliminating or changing what *isn't* working, you don't throw out the baby with the bathwater!

Here's my list for today:

Ten Things That Are Working For Me

(in no particular order)
1. One undisturbed hour with Michael every day.
2. Taking Wednesdays off as a personal day.
3. Having a special "date day" with my husband each week.
4. Relegating e-mail time to before 10 A.M. and after 10 P.M.
5. Exercising daily.
6. Having specific daily work goals and a plan to achieve them.
7. A good friend who enjoys staying with Michael when Glenn and I are out of town.
8. Work that I love.
9. A great assistant.
10. A loving, understanding, fully supportive husband.

Ten Things That Are *Not* Working For Me

(in no particular order)

1. Going to bed too late and joining an already-sleeping husband.
2. Making bad food choices.
3. How quickly the kitchen gets cluttered from mail and Michael's stuff.
4. Michael's sloppiness.
5. Spending more than I earn.
6. Working unproductively (being busy without really accomplishing my goals).
7. The mess on my desk.
8. My follow-up system.
9. Not having seen my mom recently.
10. It's after 7:00 A.M. on a school day, and I haven't finished this chapter yet!

Now I can get to work. As I study these lists, I see right away that I have a "loving, understanding, fully supportive husband" …whom I want to *keep*! My eye quickly catches #1 on my "not working" list: "Going to bed too late and joining an already-sleeping husband." Alert! At the very least, I'd better discuss with Glenn how my coming to bed late several nights each week affects him. (Whether I want to be overtired by the time I finally get to bed is another issue.)

I can't simply assume that my coming to bed late affects Glenn negatively. Perhaps he loves this alone time; I really won't know until I ask. A discussion should illuminate the situation. And if it *is* an issue for him, then I have a partner to help me consider ways to change my schedule that can benefit us both.

As I look down the list, something else jumps out at me, *Not* Working Thing #6: "Working unproductively (being busy without really accomplishing my goals)." Why would this be happening if what works for me is "Having specific daily work goals and a plan to achieve them"? Because *when* I take the time to plan my work, then I work my plan ... but I *don't do it* every day. Aha: perhaps I need to make sure to take that time every day. Here's an area where I could plan better to keep doing what works.

This simple, powerful process can be repeated weekly, monthly, or even as part of your "New Years Resolutions" to celebrate what's working and change what's not.

I invite you to join me in living a positive life by building on those experiences that feed your soul, nurture your heart and stimulate your natural intelligence; and eliminating or shifting those experiences that drain you of your God-given energy and light. Life is a grand experience. Let's enjoy the freedom to learn from it, change how we interact with it, and live it with an abundance of fullness and joy.

Words of Wisdom
"I agree to keep doing what works and change what doesn't."

If you do not change,
you can become extinct.
—Spencer Johnson[25]

When you blame others,
you give up your power to change.
—Dr. Robert Anthony

Change your thoughts and you change your world.
—Norman Vincent Peale

True wisdom is less presuming than folly.
The wise man doubteth often, and changeth his mind;
the fool is obstinate, and doubteth not;
he knoweth all things but his own ignorance.
—Akhenaton

Things do not change; we change.
—Henry David Thoreau

They always say that time changes things,
but you actually have to change them yourself.
—Andy Warhol

If you don't like something, change it.
If you can't change it, change your attitude..
—Maya Angelou

In a time of drastic change it is the learners who inherit the future.
The learned usually find themselves equipped
to live in a world that no longer exists.
—Eric Hoffer

It's not that some people have willpower and some don't.
It's that some people are ready to change and others are not.
—James Gordon, M.D.

If you don't change your beliefs, your life will be like this forever.
Is that good news?
—Douglas Noel Adams

Some people change their ways when they see the light;
others when they feel the heat.
—Caroline Schroeder

The most powerful agent of growth and transformation
is something much more basic than any technique:
a change of heart.
—John Welwood

To change one's life: Start immediately.
Do it flamboyantly. No exceptions.
—William James

Only in growth, reform, and change, paradoxically enough,
is true security to be found.
—Anne Morrow Lindbergh

It is never too late to become what you might have been.
—George Eliot

Focus on Today
I agree to keep doing what works and change what doesn't—TODAY!

Here are a few simple steps you can take to minimize struggle and maximize joy in your life by changing what's not working for you. Record your thoughts in your journal.

1. I'll make two lists: "Ten Things That Are Working For Me" and "Ten Things That Are *Not* Working For Me." I'll complete these two lists without thinking about it too much, just writing whatever first comes to mind.

2. Looking at both lists, what changes can I make that could create greater peace of mind, joy and fulfillment? What are *three positive changes* I can make in items on my "not working" list to lighten my life?

3. What one small change am I willing to make *right now* that will relieve stress and struggle and create a greater feeling of freedom and joy in my life? What am I waiting for?! (Does waiting work for me?)

4. Now that I've made this change, what's the result?

ACCEPTANCE

*God grant me the serenity
to accept the things I cannot change,
the courage to change the things I can,
and the wisdom to know the difference.*
—Reinhold Niebuhr

$\mathcal{A}$CCEPTANCE

I AGREE TO:

Listen with my heart.
Respect our differences.
Resolve conflicts directly.
Honor our choices.

The second cluster of Agreements acknowledges and celebrates our differences by agreeing to accept others for who they are. They are especially useful in dealing with the world of conflict, with graciously handling the great, glorious and often bewildering diversity of the human family.

The greatest teachers of humanity exemplified acceptance. Jesus taught to "turn the other cheek." Mahatma Gandhi and Martin Luther King, Jr. inspired us by responding to even the worst kinds of violence with acceptance of others. Nazi camp survivor and 1986 Nobel Peace Prize winner Elie Wiesel offers, ". . . there is human beauty in tolerance."[26]

These Agreements are as practical as they are timeless. You don't need to transform into a saint overnight to enjoy the rewards of acceptance. As you start to practice them, one by one, within the circumstances of everyday life, you'll be thrilled to find that you *can* practice them. They are simply new habits of behavior, as doable as drinking an extra glass of water daily for your health.

And here is the best part: the more you practice Acceptance, the more you feel the rewards of living a positive life: greater peace of mind, stronger sense of stability in your life, and improved—even *dramatically* improved—relationships with the people around you.

AGREEMENT FIVE

I agree to listen with my heart.

Listening is a magnetic and strange thing, a creative force. ... When we are listened to, it creates us, makes us unfold and expand.
—Karl A. Menninger

This Agreement applies the Golden Rule to listening: *Listen to others as you would have them listen to you.* This means listening to more than the words. To listen with your heart means listening with all your senses ... and with more than your senses, too: with your intuition, with your feelings, with your compassion.

George Benson sings, "We tried to talk it over, but the words got in the way." This Agreement means choosing not to let the words get in the way!

When we listen with our hearts as well as our minds, we can feel the pulse, the life-force that flows through each communication. It may have begun with the Word, but it doesn't stop there.

Face Value

You might ask, "Wouldn't it be easier to simply accept what people say at face value?" Well, yes and no. In fact, the expression "face value" is instructive here—because the value of someone's *face* is often significantly more than the value of his *words*.

The face (along with the breath, shoulders, position of the arms, posture of the body and other non-verbal cues) is a key to the emotions behind our words. Studies have shown that the words we speak comprise far less of our total communication than we think—even as little as seven percent! People actually pick up a great deal of what they "hear" from us, consciously or not, from all our other cues and expression.

Does this mean we should ignore people's words and make up our own assumptions about what they're really saying? Absolutely not. (The attempt to be a "mind reader" often just further muddies the communication with its assumptions!)

When I get the feeling that the person speaking means something different from the words I'm hearing, then I can simply ask for clarification. This might sound like, "I hear you saying [whatever they're saying], yet I feel some tension. Is there anything else you want to say about this?" Often simply repeating back what I've heard is enough to have her immediately clarify her meaning.

Listening Doesn't Mean Problem-Solving

I've found that it is difficult to listen respectfully when I'm thinking, "You're wrong and I'm right," or, "Oh, I get it, I know what's wrong with you," or even, "What can I do to help you?"

That last train of thought kept me from really being there for my mom for many years.

Every time my mother complained to me about something, I would immediately jump into problem-solving mode. But then, after I had (to my mind, at least) effectively problem-solved her situation, she would come back with a ready reason why my solution wouldn't work! We could easily go back and forth like this, me offering solutions and her rejecting them, until it had escalated into a bona fide shouting match.

Mom: "I have no milk in the house."

Me: "Why not?"

Mom: "My foot's been hurting too much to go to the store."

Me: "Have you asked one of your friends or neighbors to pick up some milk for you the next time they go?"

Mom: "Oh, I wouldn't bother them. Everyone has their own problems."

Me: "What about services? There must be 'helper' kinds of services in your area. Why don't you call the administration building and see who they recommend?"

Mom: "They won't know."

Me: "Then why don't you look it up in the phonebook? Let's see, what would you look under . . ."

Mom: "I'm not going to have just *anyone* come into my home!"

Me: "Arghhhhhh!"

Eventually I learned to listen—*really listen*—and to stop using what she was saying as a springboard for my own need to know better, to be right, to be an all-knowing Protector Supreme. Once I listened with my heart, what I began to hear was a woman who chooses her condition in life, just like the rest of us, someone who is utterly capable, even if she is occasionally drawn to act or speak as though she were not.

Then (and *only* then) I realized that in fact, she was rarely asking me to help her *resolve* her problems. She just wanted to speak about them, to give them voice. She wanted to be heard, that's all.

From the moment I finally understood this, our relationship blossomed. She says whatever she wants to, and I don't get hooked into feeling I'm a bad daughter if I can't fix her problems. I am off the hook, no longer struggling to come up with the answers. I now see her (and *hear* her) as entirely capable of resolving her own problems—if indeed she even perceives them as problems. My listening without judgment results in her feeling heard. Our conversations nearly always end in the most loving, empowering ways.

Now the conversation above might sound more like this:

Mom: "I have no milk in the house."

Me: "Gee, that's too bad. What's going on?"

Mom: "My foot's really been bothering me. I just don't think I can walk around the store on it."

Me: "Gosh, Mom, that must be really hard for you. What are you going to do?"

Mom: "I don't know. I see the doctor again on Tuesday. Maybe he'll have an idea. In the meantime, I'll just have to do without the milk."

Me: "That's too bad." [Time to change the subject!]

Wanting to Be Heard

I've learned that good listening often doesn't require any substantial response, only the acknowledgment of listening: "yes," "okay," "tell me more ...."

When I lived in DC, I used to drive home with my former husband each day from work, often tightly wound from a day of feeling responsible for a multi-million dollar program and the forty-some people on my team (not to mention the US Senators and their staffs who were our internal clients).

Just like my mother (and isn't *that* interesting?), I would complain and complain. And my husband would respond to me in precisely the same way that I used to respond to my mother (and isn't *that also* interesting?). Hardly letting me finish a sentence, he would jump right into solving my problems, brandishing his natural protector's sword and ready to *handle* this situation!

I would get furious—and he would be baffled. What'd he do wrong? After all, he'd just jumped to my rescue! What he didn't understand was that all I wanted was to unload, to get emotional support for my feelings, not intellectual or logistic support to attack the issue. Unfortunately, I didn't understand this either at the time, and it became a constant source of tension between us.

I know now that all I ever wanted (and all my mom ever wanted) was to be heard. Just to speak and have someone there to listen to me—not to tell me what to do, as though I were incapable of figuring it out myself.

I have plenty of opportunity to practice this Agreement. Here's a typical conversation I'd have with my young son when I had forgotten everything I know about this Agreement:

Michael: "There's no one to play with today. Everyone on the street is gone."

Me: "Why don't you call Jordie?"

Michael "I have a golf tournament this afternoon." (Mind you, it's currently 8:30 A.M.)

Me: "Why don't you play with him this morning?"

Michael: "There's not enough time. And anyway, there's no one else to play with."

Me: "What about Josh? He lives just ten minutes from here."

Michael: "I doubt he's up; he doesn't get up till ten...."

Me: "Arghhhhhh!!!"

What if, instead of trying to solve his problem for him, I simply listened with my heart? If I did, then instead of jumping in with a suggestion, I might empathize with him, "Gosh, that's tough," and then ask, "What would you like to do?"[27]

Two possibilities arise from this question. The first would be a response that lets me know it's not time for resolution. He may just need to vent his emotions: "I don't know! I can't believe all my friends on the street are gone. I have no one to play with." The second would be that he might come up with his own solution: "Maybe I'll call Lexi and see if she wants to come over . . ."—and that solution would be far more readily accepted by its creator than one I might suggest!

The best listening posture? Receptive. Open. Clear and without judgment. Ready to listen respectfully.

Listening As Empowerment

When Michael started in a new school for fourth grade, he was challenged by the social situation there. In time it became clear that it was beginning to affect his health. After verifying through tests that there were no physical ailments, we sought help from the school's counselor.

I'll never forget the day Michael met the counselor. He came home from school and exclaimed, wide-eyed, "I could tell Holly anything—*anything*. And she listened . . . Mom, she listened to *everything*!"

Carol McCall, creator of "The Empowerment of Listening" course, devotes her life to helping people learn how to truly listen so that we all can be *heard*. Her years of doctoral research have shown that we are measurably healthier, biologically and physiologically, when we feel heard.[28]

Imagine speaking with someone who has his or her complete attention on you—on truly hearing what you are saying. No judgment; no assumptions. Nowhere to go and nothing to say, just listening fully—just being there for you.

Conversations can be so much more empowering when listening with your heart.

Consider the following two scenarios. Which would be more helpful to Stephanie?

Stephanie walks in the door after a particularly grueling day at work and blurts out: "What an exhausting day!" Tom responds by trying to get to the root of the problem so he can help Stephanie feel better. He fires off one question after another: "What happened? ...Why didn't you tell him such and so? ...Why don't you make sure that gets fixed tomorrow?"

Is this helping Stephanie's exhausted state? Or worsening it?

Suppose instead of listening with a problem-solving mind, Tom listened with his heart. In this case he might ask, "Would it help for you to talk about it?" And then just listen. Stephanie may need to talk it out, or she may just need a hug. Listening with his heart, Tom could respond appropriately.

Listening is for the other person; it's not about us.

How often do others listen to you with no agenda except that of allowing you to be truly heard? How does (or would) that feel?

What if you were to do this for others?

Listening with your heart can open channels for the deepest, most meaningful communications you may ever experience; for friendships that go beyond the usual surface chatter; for teams where the members feel heard and empowered. For devoted relationships that spread love like ripples in the pond of your life ...and beyond.

Words of Wisdom
"I agree to listen with my heart."

In order that all men may be taught to speak truth,
it is necessary that likewise all should learn to hear it.
—Samuel Johnson

Everyone hears what you say.
Friends listen to what you say.
Best friends listen to what you don't say.
—Tim McGraw

I know you believe you understand
What you think I said,
But I am not sure you realize
What you heard
Is not what I meant.
—Alan Greenspan

A good listener is not only popular everywhere,
but after a while he gets to know something.
—Wilson Mizner

Gentlemen, listen to me slowly.
—Samuel Goldwyn

So when you are listening to somebody, completely, attentively,
then you are listening not only to the words,
but also to the feeling of what is being conveyed,
to the whole of it, not part of it.
—Jiddu Krishnamurti

The more faithfully you listen to the voice within you,
the better you will hear what is sounding outside.
—Dag Hammarskjöld

Difficult as it is really to listen
to someone in affliction,
it is just as difficult for him to know
that compassion is listening to him.
—Simone Weil

Courage is what it takes
to stand up and speak;
courage is also what it takes
to sit down and listen.
—Winston Churchill

As I get older, I've learned to listen to people
rather than accuse them of things.
—Po Bronson[29]

Put your ear down close to your soul
and listen hard.
—Anne Sexton

The first duty of love is to listen.
—Paul Tillich

To listen fully means to pay close attention to what is being said
beneath the words. You listen not only to the "music," but to the
essence of the person speaking. You listen not only for what
someone *knows*, but for what he or she *is*.
—Peter Senge[30]

Focus on Today
I agree to listen with my heart—TODAY!

Here are a few simple steps to improving relationships by listening with your heart.

1. Awareness of when I'm not listening with my heart is the first step in changing my listening habits. Thinking over recent interactions, I recall the following situations...

a) when I was listening with judgment:
  Example: I notice I don't even listen to Fred any more because I'm expecting to hear him whine. Maybe if I listened occasionally he would feel heard and stop whining!

b) when I was analyzing how to help the speaker:
  Example: Stephanie started complaining again. I couldn't wait to tell her how to fix her problem. I could have just said, "Gee, that's too bad. I'm sure you'll figure it out." Instead I acted like a know-it-all and didn't allow her to simply vent.

c) when I was thinking about what to say next:
  Example: While Pat was talking, I kept interrupting to say I could relate to what she was saying because of similar situations in my life. This was unnecessary, self-centered, and broke her train of thought.

2. How will I will improve my ability to listen with my heart *today?*
  Example: Quieting my mind when listening to Michael, allowing him to be fully heard without my usual judging or attempts at fixing the problem for him.

AGREEMENT SIX

I agree
to respect
our differences.

If we cannot now end our differences
at least we can help make the world safe for diversity.
—John F. Kennedy

As we grow up and venture out beyond the confines of our homes and neighborhoods, a world of exquisite diversity greets us. We alight before the multifaceted nature of the human race and add our own unique contributions to the rich tapestry of life with its magnificent discoveries, innovations and works—all created by the weaving of our differences.

What would life be like if one particular set of thoughts or one specific way of doing things were considered the *only* way?

The answer seems obvious: without different ideas, creativity would be stifled. Without fresh perspectives, problems might never be solved. Without different styles and approaches, the world would be a dreary, stultifying place with a multitude of undone tasks, unsolved problems and uninspired, unengaged people.

While this seems obvious to me in this moment, there

have been plenty of times in my life when I earnestly believed that if everyone simply did it *my way*, life would be oh-so-much-better!

As parents, we'd love our kids to do it our way. As spouses, we know life would be easier if our partner would just squeeze the toothpaste tube the same way we do. It's only natural to have the tendency to want people to do it our way. What would happen if we got our wish? Disaster!

This Agreement applies just as importantly to mundane differences as it does to the great and obvious differences that underlie wars.

The distinctions between different genders, races, cultures, political alignments and religious beliefs are of course huge and highly charged differences. Learning to respect them (even just to *accept* them) would certainly allow us to tap a source of phenomenal energy and creativity.

But equally important are the little things. In some ways, in fact, they are even *more* important, because they figure into our lives at every moment. Our lives are created not predominately in great dramatic strides, but in the moments through which we live them, day by day.

Common Goals, Different Paths

In our early days of business consulting together, I was often upset by Glenn's approach to work. I loved to be highly productive, to produce *things*. Glenn was highly creative: he loved to gestate *ideas*. It looked to me that I was working, working, working—creating PERT charts, procedural manuals, consumer guides, busy, busy, busy . . . and Glenn was walking around our client's workplace, schmoozing with the employees and top executives. Why was I doing all the work? It made me furious.

But what was Glenn really up to? Keeping in mind our common goal—*to help increase our client's productivity*—he was thinking. Every few weeks, after days and days of observing, listening and considering, his creative mind, unburdened by the busyness of my producing mind, would come up with a million-dollar idea—an idea that might be simple for our client to implement *and* pay off in increased productivity and bottom-line profits.

It took time for me to learn one of life's most important lessons: *each of us has something to contribute*. (Indeed, if my co-worker had not also been the love of my life, I might not have learned it yet!) It isn't always obvious what that "something" is, but if we respect our differences and recognize that our goals are often the same even when our methods for achieving them may differ, we will be far more likely to see what those contributions can be.

When I began to grasp the contributions Glenn was making and see how they complemented the work I was producing, this Agreement took on new meaning for me. I began to see my co-workers in a new light, looking for their gifts rather than being critical of their approaches when they differed from mine. I began to understand more deeply that there is more than one way to reach the same goal.

Unity in Diversity

Many of us work in an environment with stated common goals: a common mission shared throughout the organization and objectives for achieving that mission. Yet beyond those stated goals, it can sometimes feel like we're from different planets! Putting this Agreement into practice in the workplace allows us to tap the strength that comes from seeing the unity in diversity.

Look at any good sports team. It takes each player performing different yet complementary roles to get the ball across the goal line. It takes new ideas and innovations to evolve an organization. When I express antagonism rather than cooperation in my work team, I short-circuit the path to our common goal. Likewise, if I keep new ideas to myself (for the sake of "maintaining harmony"), I eliminate our chances for the synergy of teamwork to produce extraordinary results.

Think of the goals we share with our neighbors in our communities. To feel safe and secure; to feel loved and accepted; to have freedom of choice; to make a contribution. Do we all accomplish these goals in the same way? Of course not. I believe that the best way to be safe is to get to know my neighbors well—and others feel safe when they have loaded guns in their homes. This would not be my choice, but I have learned to respect it as theirs—after discovering that a posture of "I'm right, they're wrong" did nothing to enhance our shared goals!

One of the greatest gifts I have received in my work as a network marketer has been getting to know people whom I might never have met otherwise. I am aware of no profession with more potential for encountering diversity than network marketing. In a global business where success is not linked to background, experience or education, but rather to authenticity, enthusiasm and genuine caring about others, the opportunity for discovering differences—and making a difference—is remarkable.

Working side by side with such a diverse population was not always easy for me. Sometimes I found myself critical of different approaches and unable to contribute fully as I sat in judgment. Because I was determined to learn this profession and to rise to leadership within it, I practiced and ultimately learned to apply this Agreement with greater ease. The result has been a true gift in my life: an expanded capacity to respect differences, reap the benefits of lifelong friendships, and make contributions greater than any of us could have made by just doing it "our way."

Drinking From the Bottle

The work place is ideal for practicing this Agreement . . . but it really is true (as Dorothy said in L. Frank Baum's classic *The Wizard of Oz*) that there's *no place like home*.

In our homes, we may share a common goal for a loving, peaceful environment. For this to happen, we must find a way for each person to meet his or her own needs while not infringing on those of others.

Understanding that each of us functions differently—with different personalities, styles, needs and desires—is essential. For example, having plenty of privacy may be important to one family member, while another may thrive more on social interaction. The key is to learn how to nurture ourselves while supporting other members of the household in doing the same. This can go far to help eliminate the "victim syndrome" we so often find in our homes.

When Glenn and I co-owned our Colorado home with friends, the Revolutionary Agreements hung framed on our wall—but that didn't guarantee we always practiced them!

We had a housemate with the most annoying (to me, anyway) habit of drinking juice directly from the glass quart bottle, then returning it to the refrigerator. Whenever I caught him in the act, I would be furious and confront him. "Why don't you honor my wishes and pour your juice into a glass, like other civilized human beings!"

Looking back on this, I now ask myself, "Who made *me* the queen?" Why should he have to honor *my* wishes? If I had just accepted that this was his way and stopped pouting about it, we could have worked out a simple solution (as is the case far more often than we might imagine!).

For instance, his juice bottles could have been labeled with his name so he could drink from them to his heart's content, leaving the rest of us to pour from a separate bottle. It seems so simple now, in retrospect, but at the time I was too wrapped up in my irritation at being a victim of his ill-mannered disrespect for *my* way of doing things to see it.

In light of the problems in our world, being annoyed about a housemate drinking from a community juice bottle seems insignificant. But how many irritating little things do we let ruin our days and keep us from enjoying and contributing to a loving, peaceful life?

Our Differing Beliefs

In the larger scheme of things, nowhere is it more important to *respect differences* than when it comes to our most strongly-held beliefs.

We may share a common goal to experience the deepest possible relationship with our Creator, yet the words, beliefs and methods we choose for experiencing that spiritual relationship are multitudinous. Respecting different beliefs has opened up many possibilities for me to understand, appreciate and strengthen my own relationship to the Source of Life.

We have seen what thousands of years of "I'm right, you're wrong" have accomplished. How many people have been killed for their beliefs? How many are still being killed today? Isn't it due time that we citizens of the world evolved from killing each other for our beliefs to respecting our differences?

Imagine if our children, instead of saying to each other, "You talk funny," or, "You're stupid," learned to say thoughtfully, "That's a different way of thinking about that."

Where do they get their prejudices from? If not from our own households, then from the collective thought to which we all contribute. What if the prevailing thought in our homes changed? How might that affect your home life ...? And beyond? What if our attitudes and the way we live our lives affected our neighbors and others around us *positively*?

I remember remarking to a friend one day after having her daughter in my car, "Your daughter sure likes to talk badly about other children." She replied, "I guess she learns that from me. I have a tendency to complain in front of her about people I think are jerks." I was struck by the woman's honesty and self-awareness. Many people are as unaware of the judgments they carry (and broadcast) as of the air they breathe.

Since he was six years old, I have told our son that one of the really cool things about being human is that we can believe whatever we choose. So why not choose to believe in those things that are positive and loving, those things that foster the betterment of humanity and the world? When sharing the idea that everyone can believe whatever they want, I would explain that some people choose to believe that *their* belief is the *only* truth . . . and that's okay, too, because that's *their* belief.

"Respect" Doesn't Mean "Agree With"

This Agreement is yet another facet of the Golden Rule: "Respect others the way you would wish them to respect you." But it's important to be very clear about this distinction: Does "respect" mean "agree with"? No.

While I don't agree with President Bush for initiating war with another country, I respect that we have different methods of achieving similar goals: personal freedom and peace in our world.

Do I know if his method is better or worse than mine? Not really. There is no way to know, in the short term. All I can do is respect our differences and continue to speak my truth, with compassion; to make a contribution with every word I speak and every act I make; to never give up on something I believe in, while respecting the rights of those who believe differently.

I hope you will join me in respecting our differences, and as a result, find a new level of inner peace while contributing to the creation of a peaceful world.

Words of Wisdom
"I agree to respect our differences."

If civilization is to survive, we must cultivate
the science of human relationships—
the ability of all people of all kinds
to live together and to work together
in the same world—at peace.
—Franklin D. Roosevelt

Before God we are all equally wise—and equally foolish.
—Albert Einstein

Opinions founded on prejudice are always
sustained with the greatest violence.
—Francis Jeffrey

Everything we shut our eyes to, everything we run away from,
everything we deny, denigrate or despise,
serves to defeat us in the end.
What seems nasty, painful, evil,
can become a source of beauty, joy and strength,
if faced with an open mind.
Every moment is a golden one
for him who has the vision
to recognize it as such.
—Henry Miller

There is divine beauty in learning,
just as there is human beauty in tolerance.
—Elie Wiesel

The essence of our effort to see that every child has a chance
must be to assure each an equal opportunity,
not to become equal, but to become different—
to realize whatever unique potential of
body, mind and spirit he or she possesses.
—John Martin Fischer

As we grow as unique persons,
we learn to respect the uniqueness of others.
—Robert H. Schuller

Have a dialogue between the two opposing parts
and you will find that they always start out fighting each other
until we come to an appreciation of difference . . .
a oneness and integration of the two opposing forces.
Then the civil war is finished, and your energies are ready
for your struggle with the world.
—Frederick Salomon Perls

I believe in God, only I spell it Nature.
—Frank Lloyd Wright

Believing ourselves to be possessors of absolute truth
degrades us: we regard every person whose way of thinking
is different from ours as a monster and a threat
and by so doing turn our own selves into
monsters and threats to our fellows.
—Octavio Paz

It is never too late to give up your prejudices.
—Henry David Thoreau

Focus on Today
I agree to respect our differences—TODAY!

Here are two simple steps to begin releasing unproductive drama in your life and fostering an empowering environment in which people feel free to express their true Selves. Record your thoughts in your journal.

1. Who are those people in my life with whom I have most difficulty? And what is it that bugs me about him or her?
   Example: MM, because of his know-it-all attitude.

2. For every reason I listed above about what bugs me, what might be a positive aspect of that same behavior? And how I can change my attitude from disdain to appreciation?
   Example: The truth is, MM actually does know a lot! He could be a good resource. And what I can appreciate about him is that he freely and unselfishly shares what he knows.

AGREEMENT SEVEN

I agree to resolve conflicts directly.

It's not a problem that we have a problem.
It's a problem if we don't deal with the problem.
—Mary Kay Utecht

Living in a world of diversity, it is inevitable that conflicts occur. "Respecting our differences" doesn't mean ignoring or glossing over conflicts; on the contrary, it means treating *them* with respect, too. This Agreement asks us to handle such problems directly, which means with speed and compassion and always—*always*—by speaking directly with the person with whom we have the problem.

Why do we so often tend not to do this? Before I experienced the peace of mind that results from practicing this Agreement, I used to do anything I could to avoid confrontation. If I got provoked, I would first solidify my position (proving I was right) by making the rounds and telling "my side" of the issue to people I trusted to build up support for my case. Hey, there's strength in numbers, right?

Wrong. In fact, when it comes to resolving conflict, I've

learned that greater numbers only compound the problem. In fact, when it comes to resolving conflict, there is often *weakness* in numbers! Years of practicing this Agreement have taught me that strength lies in direct communication, with compassion, as soon as possible. Going directly to speak with the person with whom I can resolve the conflict minimizes unnecessary drama and stress.

Consider my conflict with my friend Linda which I described in Agreement Two. The way she handled this was all too common: rather than speak directly with me, she complained to a friend. This problem, left on its own, would likely have only escalated and never gotten cleared up. Our mutual friend had encouraged Linda to come speak with me about it. When she didn't, our friend brought it to me, which in turn enabled me to go speak directly with Linda and open up the possibility of resolution.

I still step outside this Agreement from time to time. When that happens, when I catch myself complaining about a third person, I am moved to go clean it up immediately. I may call the person I spoke with and say, "I really shouldn't have talked to you about X; I'm going to be calling that person directly, and I hope you'll do me the favor of not passing on what I said to anybody else." And then I go speak directly with the source of my issue.

I've said that embracing these Agreements and living a positive life takes courage. Of all the Agreements, this one can feel like it takes the most courage of all. And, as with all sincere acts of courage, the rewards are well worth it.

Dismantling the Rumor Mill

The workplace is a notorious hotbed for gossip, yet interestingly enough, I've found this Agreement is invariably welcomed in the workplace with tremendous enthusiasm. When offered a way to dismantle the fickle and destructive institution of the rumor mill by adopting a more constructive way to behave, people embrace it with open arms.

The next time you hear an upsetting rumor at work, what if instead of passing on the bad news and your upset feelings to your co-workers, you instead went directly and immediately to the source of the issue and said, "I just heard X, and wanted to know whether or not it's true."

I have done this dozens of times. Sometimes I hear the response, "No, it's certainly *not* true!" and then have the privilege and delight of sharing the good news with my co-workers. Sometimes I will learn that yes, in fact, the rumor is true. I can then find out exactly why this is so first hand, with all the salient details and perspectives, which in turn enables me to share with my co-workers the reasons and the truth behind the rumor.

I heard once through the grapevine that "Jack," a friend and member of my network marketing organization, had begun working for a different (and competing) company. My first angry impulse was to call the key people in our organization up and down the line, as well as key people at the corporate offices, and tell everyone of Jack's traitorous acts. In my shocked disbelief, my mind scrambled to come up with a plan for researching the competing company so we could map out a defensive strategy for keeping Jack's people from leaving our company and joining the new one with which he had so blackheartedly aligned himself.

Luckily for all involved, the essence of this Agreement kicked in before I took any action.

Instead, I sent Jack an e-mail: "I just heard that you were leading a training call for another network marketing company. Can you enlighten me?" He wrote back, "I have been hired by this new network marketing company to teach their associates my cold-calling techniques. I am getting paid to do this, and yes, they have also given me a position in their network as part of my compensation. However, other than the teaching I've been hired to do, I am pursuing no other income from this new company. My allegiance always has been and always will be with the company we both love."

It took only minutes to go to the source and resolve this issue to my complete satisfaction. How long would it have taken me to clean up the damage I could have caused had I passed on the rumor that Jack had abandoned ship?

The Camel and the Straw

In this Agreement, the word "directly" has two meanings: it means going straight to the person involved and speaking with him or her—and it also means *as soon as possible*. One of the keys to successful problem-solving is timing, and that applies here.

We don't want to engage a contributor to a problem until we are calm enough to listen with our heart, yet at the same time, we also don't want to wait too long to deal with it. Here's an analogy that has helped me remember to resolve problems as quickly as possible:

Every time something upsets you, imagine that you are taking a rock and dropping it into a pack that you wear on your back at all times. Small upsets may be only small rocks ("No big deal…"), but after years of accumulating them, that pack can get pretty heavy. Once you reach a certain point, adding even one more rock, no matter how small—even a pebble!—can finally throw you completely off balance.

That pebble is what people call "the straw that broke the camel's back."

Have you ever said something you thought was minor, yet the person you said it to came back with a *major* response, one that seemed way out of proportion to your slight transgression? Even if it seemed like a pebble to you, what you gave that person may well have been more than their heavy backpack could carry…the last straw.

We may think (as I have many times), "This is so small, so insignificant—it's not worth the trouble to bring it up and hash it over again ..." Perhaps not; but by *not* resolving it at the earliest opportunity, we've chosen to add a rock or two to the heavy accumulation of emotional baggage in our lifelong collection.

The Power of Multiple Agreements

The practice of any one Agreement leads naturally to the others. This is especially obvious with this Agreement.

Before going to speak with the person to *resolve the conflict directly* (Agreement Seven), stop and *look within at your reaction* (Agreement Three). Examining your own reactions and emotional responses to the situation first can go a long way to removing any excessive emotional charge on the issue for you, and you may find yourself in far better shape to present the issue clearly and dispassionately—if the issue isn't already fully resolved from within.

When you do go speak to the person, you'll want to *speak your truth, with compassion* (Agreement Two). It is a wonderful feeling to have the habit of asking ourselves, when faced with an emotional issue, "How can I speak my truth—with compassion—in this moment?" rather than simply reacting: "All right—how can I unload this lifetime of rocks *right now*?!"

And as you problem-solve, you'll be *listening with your heart* (Agreement Five).

Do you see how in this one situation, you can use not one, not two, but four of these Revolutionary Agreements to transform the situation?

Under One Roof

This Agreement may be the reason our family was able to live under the same roof for so many years with my best friend,

Gail and her husband, Gregory. We did this initially for purely economic reasons. We all traveled extensively, and this arrangement afforded us all a magnificent home to return to between trips. Soon, though, we came to enjoy the camaraderie of built-in neighbors and friends with whom we shared our daily bread.

Quite a few people were surprised (some might have said "amazed") that we were able to share our home for thirteen years and still successfully remain friends. How did we create a harmonious environment for four—and eventually, with the addition of our son, Michael, for five? After all, doesn't "familiarity breed contempt"?

The answer was simply that to the best of our abilities, we lived by these Agreements—and this particular Agreement was the arch stone. Whenever the slightest issue or potential bone of contention arose, we would address it in the moment, or at least as soon as possible once upset feelings had a chance to calm down. We didn't gossip. We didn't take sides. We didn't complain to someone else about an issue with another. We took our issues directly to the person or persons with whom we could resolve it—*always*.[31]

Nothing seems sadder to me than a husband or wife walking away from a marriage and home without so much as a whisper about why. What has happened here? Years of tossing small (and sometimes not so small) rocks into that backpack until it got so heavy it felt impossible to carry. If only he had talked with her when the issues first came up . . . perhaps they would have found an early resolution. If only she had felt empowered to speak her truth...perhaps they would be celebrating their 50th anniversary together instead of living apart.

This Agreement can save marriages, homes and countless other human relationships. Indeed, it may be what's needed to save the world.

How to Broach the Issue

Because it can be difficult to begin the communication, I have learned some starter phrases that work for me, regardless of the issue. Feel free to use one or more of them:

"Something doesn't feel right."

"Why did you say that to me? That didn't feel good."

"Something just happened that doesn't feel good to me."

"This isn't working for me."

In our situation, with Glenn, me, Gail and Gregory all living under one roof, here is the kind of exchange we typically found ourselves having in the spirit of this Agreement:

"Marian—what can we do about your leaving the dishes in the sink? We've talked about this before, but you keep slipping into old habits." As the reigning drama queen of our household, I might groan, "Ahh...I've been *so* busy today!" The silence would let me know that Gregory wasn't accepting the invitation to join my pity party. With no other way out, I would move to resolution: "I'll take care of it in about an hour, when I finish what I'm doing, okay? And I'll try to stay on top of it in the future."

By being vulnerable, not having the answers, not controlling the situation, but simply stating, "Something isn't working here," we often found we could open the door to collaboration and co-creation. Of course, it helps when the person we're talking with knows this Agreement, too!

What If They Come To Me?

This Agreement takes on an interestingly different hue in cases where someone else comes to you with a complaint, rather than taking it to the person it involves. You don't want to refuse to hear your friend or co-worker...but you also don't want to support third-party, indirect communication. What can you do?

My first response would be to listen with your heart. In fact, it can sometimes be wise and helpful to seek counsel from a good friend or an impartial observer before addressing concerns we have with another. That advisor may be able to help us clarify our own motivations and coach us on how to communicate our upsets in a mature way.

It's only natural to want to be there for our friends and teammates when they are upset. A friend in need is a friend indeed. So we listen with our heart to their complaints—before gently and firmly redirecting them to the appropriate person: "Have you talked with her about it? ... Would you like to resolve it?"

For the good of all concerned, there may come a time when we need to draw a line. If we continue to allow our friends and colleagues to cry on our shoulder time and time again and never address the problem directly, we are helping them to perpetuate a destructive cycle.

Granted, it might not be a simple problem that can be addressed with a simple conversation (although it might have been simple years ago, when it first arose). In its later stages, when a conflict has had time to grow complex and deeply entrenched, professional help might be needed—a therapist or a mediator, perhaps. The best advice we can offer our friends and team members is to move their conversation to the people with whom resolution can be found, and take it from there.

Let's not let another day go by without taking this tremendous opportunity to enrich our lives by resolving problems directly and speaking our truth—with compassion. Let's not put another rock into our already heavy emotional backpacks. Indeed, let's begin to take those rocks out, one at a time, read the labels on them, and settle unresolved issues that are still festering from some past conflict. Join me in lightening our load and becoming models for others to do the same. This is Revolutionary Leadership.

Words of Wisdom
"I agree to resolve conflicts directly."

The best way to escape from a problem is to solve it.
—Alan Saporta

It is one of man's curious idiosyncrasies
to create difficulties for the pleasure of resolving them.
—Joseph De Maistre

A rumor without a leg to stand on
will get around some other way.
—John Tudor

The things most people want to know about
are usually none of their business.
—George Bernard Shaw

Whoever gossips to you
will gossip about you.
—Spanish proverb

If we are too busy, if we are carried away every day
by our projects, our uncertainty, our craving,
how can we have the time to stop and look deeply
into the situation—our own situation, the situation of our
beloved one, the situation of our family and of our community,
and the situation of our nation and of the other nations?
—Thich Nhat Hanh

Peace is not the absence of conflict
but the presence of creative alternatives for responding to
conflict—alternatives to passive or aggressive responses,
alternatives to violence.
—Dorothy Thompson

Man must evolve for all human conflict
a method which rejects revenge, aggression and retaliation.
The foundation of such a method is love.
—Martin Luther King, Jr.

We have war when at least one of the parties to a conflict
wants something more than it wants peace.
—Jeanne J. Kirkpatrick

A good manager doesn't try to eliminate conflict;
he tries to keep it from wasting the energies of his people.
If you're the boss and your people fight you openly
when they think that you are wrong—that's healthy.
—Robert Townsend

The greatest conflicts are not between two people
but between one person and himself.
—Garth Brooks

When I'm working on a problem, I never think about beauty.
I think only how to solve the problem. But when I have finished,
if the solution is not beautiful, I know it is wrong.
—R. Buckminster Fuller

Focus on Today
I agree to resolve conflicts directly—TODAY!

Here are a few courageous steps you can take to free yourself from unnecessary drama and struggle in your life. Record your thoughts in your journal.

1. I'm going to take the backpack of unresolved conflict rocks off my back today—hooray! Then I'll list and label as many rocks as I can:

   Example: The day Mom said I looked fat . . . when I heard that my friend L talked badly about me behind my back . . . when my co-worker AB didn't do his part of our project and I had to do more work than I should have.

2. I'll pick *one* of those labeled rocks to get rid of right now! First I'll write a letter to the person whose name is on the label, saying everything I want to say to that person—really get everything off my chest. Then I'll destroy the letter with a little ceremony to celebrate lightening my load. The true test will be the next time I see or even think about that person: will the strength of that issue have diminished—or even disappeared altogether? If this works for me, I'll do it with another rock every day until my backpack is empty and I'm feeling lighter and freer!

3. *Today*, as soon as I notice a problem, issue or complaint I have with someone else, I'll express how I'm feeling (speak my truth, with compassion). I'll speak only for myself and about myself and my own needs, and refrain from blaming the other.

   Example: "I'm feeling tired tonight. Do you have the energy to help me prepare dinner?" Not: "You never help with dinner and it's driving me crazy!"

AGREEMENT EIGHT

I agree
to honor
our choices.

When we acknowledge that all of life is sacred and that each act is an act of choice and therefore sacred, then life is a sacred dance lived consciously each moment. When we live at this level, we participate in the creation of a better world.
—Scout Cloud Lee

Have you ever beaten yourself up emotionally for a decision you made? Have you ever been harshly critical of others' choices? Does this leave you feeling positive, upbeat and creative—or negative, distressed and counter-productive?

Honor our choices. If we lived just this one Agreement, our lives would change dramatically. These three words, deeply absorbed into our being, could dispel a lifetime of blame and shame.

Honor our choices. Know that we all make the best decisions and choices we are capable of in the moment we make them.

There Are No "Bad" Decisions

Think back to a decision you made in the past, a decision you later regretted. In retrospect, you may very well think of this as a "bad decision." Perhaps you have even felt that it ruined your life. Was it marrying the wrong person and being miserable through all your years together? Taking a job that was so stressful you got sick? Choosing travel over time at home with your children who grew up so suddenly?

Now, consider the moment in which you made your "bad" decision. If you could reconstruct that instant in its every aspect and circumstance, including every thought and experience leading up to it, would you see yourself intentionally choosing something you knew would hurt you? Or would you observe yourself choosing a path that you believed was the very best decision for you, based on everything you knew and everything you were feeling at that moment?

Rather than enveloping yourself in blame or regret, acknowledge that this was a choice you made—and *honor your choice*.

Do you recall Agreement Four? "I agree to keep doing what works and change what doesn't." It's also important not to condemn yourself for those things you now decide need changing. You're going to change them, and that's good—and even as you change them, *honor your choices*. Do this and you'll remove yourself from the burdensome path of self-judgment. Instead of focusing on what you *should* have done, you'll be taking action (making another choice) to move yourself forward.

Certainly for those of us in second marriages, it can be tempting to call a first marriage a "bad decision." But what good does that do? I could easily wallow in the feeling that I made a wrong choice, bemoaning the fact that "I wasted ten years of my life!" and castigating myself for not recognizing and leaving an unhealthy relationship sooner.

Or I can choose to uplift myself by focusing on the positive aspects of my ex-husband and of our relationship, acknowledging the value of what I learned in that relationship that serves me even today.

It's often not easy to have this kind of clarity in the midst of overwhelming emotion, yet it is precisely this ability to lift ourselves out of harsh judgment (both of others and of ourselves) that opens up more space in our lives for joy.

For many years following my father's death, I suffered because of the way I clung to him in his final days. Rather than blessing him, celebrating his life and letting him know we'd all be okay if it was his time to go, all I could do was literally "hold on for dear life." His passing while I desperately sought a way to keep him alive haunted me for a long time. Oh, if only I had been able to offer him sweetness and love in his final hours, rather than feeling fearful of his approaching death and bitter towards the doctors, whom I blamed.

Looking back some years later, I realized that losing Dad had been a new experience for me. I'd never lost a parent before and wasn't prepared—and I did the best I knew how under the circumstances. I was on a mission to save his life, and I had a learning experience. Once I could see this, I could now make new and different decisions about how I would relate to the eventual passing of my mother.

I was never able to speak with my father about the inevitability of his death. Today I can speak openly and lovingly with my mother about hers.

"Mom, do you ever think about the fact that you are closer to the end of your life than to the beginning?" I asked one day. Her answer: "No ... and you wouldn't think so, either, if you saw how I shopped. I'm buying things that will last me another fifty years!"

I no longer take my parent for granted, as if she will go on living forever. I take care to express my love daily, and I will continue doing so until the day that she dies. This is something I learned from the choices I made—and that I now honor—with my dad.

Perhaps the greatest choice we have is how we feel about our present circumstances—and this includes how we feel about those choices and decisions that have led to those circumstances. Rather than judging ourselves based on the outcome of our decisions, what if we loved ourselves (and others) for the courage to make the choices we make every day?

We do the best that we can. You. Your spouse. Your boss. Your parents, your children, your neighbors…everyone with whom you come into contact. We all make the very best possible choices or decisions of which we are capable in that moment.

There Are No "Mistakes"

I used to be very hard on myself. My long-time need for others to like me and think I excelled at whatever I was doing created a tremendous amount of stress in my life.

One day my favorite boss and mentor, Mary Ruth, called me into her office and asked, "Marian, do you expect your husband to be perfect?" Puzzled as to why she might be asking this question, I replied honestly, "No, of course not."

Then she asked, "Do you expect the managers who report to you to be perfect?" Ahh … now I thought I understood. Someone must have made a big mistake, and this was her way of gently letting me know about it. I answered truthfully, "No, of course not."

Then came her punch line: "Then why do you think *you* have to be perfect?"

I learned from the ensuing conversation that my pattern of self-criticism was not only unhealthy for me, it also created stress and unnecessary drama for others in my workplace.

Now, many years later, that stressed-out sense of always needing to feel perfect is gone. In its place is the contentment of knowing and living this Revolutionary Agreement to the best of my ability. When I embody this Agreement, I spend less time beating myself up and more time learning from my decisions. I spend less time blaming myself and others and more time accepting and moving on.

James Burke tells a wonderful story of his early days at Johnson & Johnson. One day, after Burke's first major project as head of a new products division had failed, the Chairman General called him into his office and asked, "Are you the one who just cost us all that money?"

Expecting to be fired, Burke could only nod his head glumly: yes, he was the one. The Chairman General's next words shocked him:

"Well, I just want to congratulate you. If you are making mistakes, that means you are making decisions and taking risks. And we won't grow unless you take risks."[32]

At the Neenan Company in Ft. Collins, Colorado, a gong reverberates through the halls of the workplace when someone notices a mistake. When the gong sounds, the staff all eagerly ask one another, "What was the mistake?"—so that they can learn from it. It's their culture to celebrate what they call "learning experiences" rather than punishing what other companies would call "mistakes."

Thinking of myself as a "learner" and using the term "learning experience" in place of the word "mistake" has helped me to embody this Agreement. Try it—it may do the same for you!

Only God Has God's Perspective

Some days I'm better at practicing this Agreement than others.

I've often found myself in situations where I would be tempted to say, "There goes Glenn again, off to lunch with his buddies—eating unhealthy food and spending money unnecessarily when there's food in our refrigerator." When I noticed my judgment, I thought of this Agreement, and was able to say instead, "Isn't it great that Glenn has such good friends and that they so enjoy having lunch together?"

Yesterday I saw a car speed by my house. Reflexively filled with judgment, my first thought was, "What a maniac! Why doesn't he slow down—he could hurt somebody!"

Then this Agreement kicked in. My next thought was, "What if he's in a rush to get to a sick child?" Or for that matter, what if there were some other reason, albeit one unknown to me, that it was imperative this man move quickly? I'll never really know.

And that's exactly the point: most of the time, we *don't* know and *can't* know why people make the choices they do.

Many years ago, a wise speaker made a life-changing impact on me when he said, "Unless you know a person's complete history, all that he has experienced in the past and all that is intended for his future, there is no way you can judge him for what he does today."

It is clear to me that only God can see from this perspective. Meanwhile, here on Earth, we can *honor our choices*.

Acceptance and Forgiveness

At the core of this Agreement, at its very deepest meaning, a question arises concerning forgiveness: "If I truly accept someone for who she is, with no judgment, then is there any need for forgiveness?"

In our culture, we spend so much time exploring the value of forgiveness. What would it be like if we simply practiced acceptance? Now that's revolutionary!

Even with the best of intentions, our decisions never stand alone. Every choice connects with others' choices to render an outcome that is beyond our knowing. As Stephen Covey so aptly puts it, "While we are free to choose our actions, we are not free to choose the consequences of those actions."[33]

I invite you to go through your day today noticing the well from which your decisions spring. Begin to honor yourself for every choice you make. Enjoy a feeling of excited anticipation: "What will happen as a result of this decision, as it mingles with all other decisions converging in the collective consciousness?"

As we release our judgments and accept that we are all making the best possible choices we are capable of in this moment, we are contributing to a revolution of genuinely epic proportion. We are changing lives; indeed, we are changing the world.

Words of Wisdom
"I agree to honor our choices."

Hindsight is always twenty-twenty.
—Billy Wilder

Honor isn't about making the right choices.
It's about dealing with the consequences.
—Midori Koto[34]

Whatever humans have learned had to be learned
as a consequence only of trial and error experience.
Humans have learned only through mistakes.
—Buckminster Fuller[35]

Great Spirit, help me never to judge another
until I have walked in his moccasins.
—Sioux Indian prayer

In any moment of decision
the best thing you can do is the right thing,
the next best thing is the wrong thing,
and the worst thing you can do is nothing.
—Theodore Roosevelt

Nothing is more difficult, and therefore more precious,
than to be able to decide.
—Napoleon Bonaparte

There is simply no such thing as a correct decision.
Life is far too complicated for that.
—Tom Peters[36]

If a woman has to choose between
catching a fly ball and saving an infant's life,
she will choose to save the infant's life
without even considering if there are men on base.
—Dave Barry

If you have made mistakes, even serious mistakes—
there is always another chance for you...
you may have a fresh start any moment you choose,
for this thing we call failure is not the falling down,
but the staying down.
—Mary Pickford

The nice thing about standards is that
there are so many of them to choose from.
—Andrew S. Tanenbaum

No man chooses evil because it is evil;
he only mistakes it for happiness, the good he seeks.
—Mary (Shelley) Wollstonecraft

All our final decisions are made in a state of mind
that is not going to last.
—Marcel Proust

Choose your love,
Love your choice.
—Thomas S. Monson

Focus on Today
I agree to honor our choices—TODAY!

Here are a few steps that will start you down the path of non-judgment and acceptance that leads to unconditional love. Record your thoughts in your journal.

1. I'll explore the reasons I made what I now consider "bad decisions."

> DECISION: *I spent two years in therapy with my spouse.* REASON: *I thought it would keep us together.* OUTCOME: *He left me anyway! At the time of the decision, did I make the best choice I knew how?*

2. I'm going to celebrate every "mistake" I make today, consciously reframing each one as a fortunate learning experience.

> WHAT HAPPENED: *I was so busy I didn't take my supplements today. I was tired and cranky by day's end.* LEARNING: *Make nutrition a priority, especially when under a deadline! It helps me to feel better and be more creative and productive.*

3. I'll take time to consider whether I have any judgments about others' choices that negatively affect my day and block my creative flow and ability to make a positive contribution.

> *Example: Tracy decided not to do the work needed to earn the cruise incentive. How lazy she is!*

Then I'll ask myself: "Do I know this person's complete history, including all the experiences that brought this person to this point? What positive reason might have inspired this person to make that decision?"

> *Example: I have no idea what's going on in Tracy's life. Perhaps her three kids need her more than she feels she needs the money she'd earn by revving up her business. (Maybe she gets seasick!)*

GRATITUDE

To speak gratitude is courteous and pleasant,
to enact gratitude is generous and noble,
but to live gratitude is to touch Heaven.
—Johannes A. Gaertner

GRATITUDE

I AGREE TO:

Give and receive thanks.
See the best in myself and others.
Look for blessings in disguise.
Lighten up!

The word *gratitude* shares the same root as do the words "grace" and "gracious." To be "grateful" means to be full of pleasure and steeped in grace; to be awash in a sense of delight at all the wonders, the blessings, the deliriously, deliciously exquisite joys of life unfolding on all sides.

The last set of Agreements are all aspects of this "state of grace."

Gratitude has to do with developing the habit of seeing what's right rather than what's wrong; of seeing the best in everything around us.

Does this mean blinding ourselves to "the realities" of life? On the contrary, it means *shining our light* onto those realities even as we embrace them. It is no coincidence that the last Agreement is to "lighten up." All four Agreements in this third group have to do with being *delighted* in and about your life.

The final message of the Revolutionary Agreements is beautifully expressed in this passage from the Kabbalah:

First we receive the light;
Then we impart the light;
Thus we repair the world.

AGREEMENT NINE

I agree to give and receive thanks.

There is more hunger for love and appreciation in this world than for bread.
—Mother Teresa[37]

Voicing appreciation for others is helpful; letting people know when you see them doing their best encourages them to keep on going for it. But being *truly grateful* for another's actions and contributions . . . now that's life-changing! My friend Vivian lives by this credo: "People may forget what you said or what you did, but they will always remember how you made them feel."

Finding Gratitude in the Moment...

In my home, our family has long had the habit of giving thanks for all the mundane, everyday actions and events in our lives—even those we long ago came to expect. In so doing, we touch each other's hearts and create greater joy and fulfillment in our lives.

On a typical morning, while I prepare a hot breakfast for Michael, he empties the dishwasher—two opportunities for thank-you's. I prepare his lunch and he feeds our dog, Boomer—two more opportunities. He cleans up the kitchen table before I drive him to school—more opportunities. "Thanks, Mom. See you after school!"

"Thanks for the great breakfast you made me this morning . . ."

"Thanks for taking out the garbage . . ."

"Thank you for listening . . ."

"Thank you for being here for me . . ."

"Thank you for being you . . ."

". . . I appreciate you!"

I've mentioned several times that practicing these Agreements takes courage. True enough for the others—but I think this Agreement is the *easiest* to practice. Once you start finding reasons to say *Thank you*, it soon becomes almost impossible to stop, because you start seeing them everywhere!

When he was younger, Michael would end his day by lighting a candle in his darkened room. The light signified the light of God; Glenn and I would sit by his bed and each of us would express our gratitude for everything we could think of.

From morning until night, from the people in our lives to the Source of our lives, we live in an abundance of opportunities to feel and express appreciation. It is magical to fill our lives with countless moments of gratitude both by *noticing* them more and by *creating* more of them.

...and For Things To Come

Having the fullness of gratitude for everything around us is a wonderful feeling, yet there is a still deeper level of gratitude: giving thanks for what we *don't yet have*.

Can you imagine how much better we'd all feel if instead of worrying about something, we celebrated and felt gratitude for those outcomes we desire and can picture in our minds? In fact, being grateful for something we envision makes it that much more likely that we will actually experience it—that it *will* happen. Great athletes and successful professionals know how to visualize the future and pour their emotions into the imagined outcome as though it had just happened.

In our training program, "VisionWorks: Setting Your Sights on Success!," Glenn and I guide teams through envisioning their ideal work situation from an imaginary future vantage point, looking back in time to celebrate extraordinary accomplishment. With an uplifting feeling of gratitude for having reached the pinnacle of success, each team member imagines the workplace in its highest possible state, from the physical environment to the way in which they communicate with one another. They then share their visions with each other; all is captured on flip charts around the room; priorities are set; and teams self-select to implement the changes needed to create their combined vision.

This groundbreaking process (which Glenn initiated in the 1970s) produces results that simply wouldn't be possible without the ability to feel gratitude for something that hasn't yet happened—to become, as Norman Vincent Peale termed it, "possibilitarians."

The act of envisioning and feeling gratitude is sometimes enough in itself to create far-reaching changes, even without additional action. For many, picturing and being grateful for their own healthy bodies has helped to heal themselves from life-threatening illnesses.

Before Michael's gymnastics meets, we would help him reduce his anxiety by using positive imagery. We would picture him enjoying the camaraderie of his teammates, laughing alongside them and cheering each other on. His fear invariably turned to excitement.

One of my mentors, best friends and business partners, Marion Culhane, taught me this through practical application:

what we focus our attention and intention on is what we get. If we focus on lack, then lack is what we'll have; if we focus on anticipated failures, then failures will more likely befall us. And if we focus on gratitude, then that's what we'll experience. Which would you prefer?

True Wealth

I overheard a conversation with Mother Teresa that affected me profoundly. Responding to a despairing comment about the poor people she served, she said, "Some people I have worked with in impoverished environments are not as poor as some of the wealthiest people of the West. Their richness is of the heart and the Spirit; their love of God gives them peace of mind."

This richness she spoke of is accessible to each of us, right in this moment, and in every moment. The doorway to achieving it is the feeling and expression of gratitude.

People often devote more energy to bringing down other people than to building them up. From the time we are teased (or tease others) on the playground to the day we join in the gossip round the water cooler at work, we are immersed in a culture that fosters negativity. In the midst of such a societal norm, it takes character and emotional fortitude to express appreciation for others—with rewards well worth the effort.

I love what classical singer Marian Anderson, who achieved great success despite unspeakable racial discrimination throughout her life, had to say: "As long as you keep a person down, some part of you has to be down there to hold him down, so it means you cannot soar as you might otherwise."[38]

Imagine a room full of people putting down others, and another room next door filled with people expressing their appreciation for others. If you were to measure the volume of joy and fulfillment in the two rooms, how do you think they might compare? Which group do you choose to be in?

Receiving Thanks

Receiving thanks is as important as giving thanks, for one cannot exist fully without the other. Yet while most of us are taught how to say "Thank you," it is a rare thing indeed for people to be taught how to receive thanks.

Can you remember the last time you thanked someone, only to have that person respond by looking away and changing the subject, or making a joke, or saying, "Oh, it was nothing." Do you remember how this felt? By minimizing or deflecting your appreciation, they short-circuited it. In a very real sense, they *denied* it. Most likely they did so without any intention of dishonoring your thanks; it's just how we were raised. But intentionally or not, in that moment your expression of thanks *was* dishonored.

This Agreement asks us to accept acknowledgment graciously and fully. Receiving thanks means *letting it in*. It means looking into the eyes of the one appreciating us, uncrossing our arms, smiling and breathing in the acknowledgment. "You're welcome" may be the appropriate response, or "It was my pleasure," if that's the truth. Or perhaps, "Thank you for your acknowledgment," spoken from your heart. The exact words matter less; the spirit of it means everything. In so doing, the gift is returned and the cycle of gratitude is allowed to complete.

Thanking Ourselves

As little as we are taught to receive thanks, even more rarely are we taught to appreciate and thank *ourselves* for the contributions we make.

As adults, we are taught that our leader is responsible for acknowledging our work. Can you imagine a boss who would say, "Be sure to let me know when you feel you've done something worthy of my notice!"? Yet that's just what Glenn and I have done.

When hiring staff for one of our consulting jobs, we asked a young applicant if he could accept our "Team Agreements." At the time, this particular Agreement read, "I agree to take responsibility for acknowledging myself." He was adamant that this was not his responsibility: "As your employee, I think it's *your* job to acknowledge me."

I told him, "We're usually on top of noticing and acknowledging our team members' contributions—but what if we miss something? What if you were to make a contribution that saved our client thousands of dollars . . . and no one noticed? How would you feel? Why feel unappreciated for even one moment? Why not celebrate your successes by claiming your contribution with joy: 'Guess what I've done!' or even, 'Hey! I deserve a medal for this one!'"

This young man's dilemma is not uncommon. We often go about life feeling unappreciated for our contributions, yet without the know-how or permission to make known our successes.

With practice, this Agreement can become easy and fun.

Sitting at the dining room table at a great meal prepared by *moi*, I can easily say something like, "I'd love to get some acknowledgment for this meal. It took hours of loving preparation and only minutes to eat!" I don't feel the need to do this often, but if I feel even the tiniest twinge of, *They have no idea how hard I worked on this* . . . , I ask for acknowledgment.

And the funny thing is, when I've asked with a loving heart, I've never been denied it.

When we appreciate something, it *appreciates in value*. Imagine all of the aspects of our lives—relationships, finances, work, health and more—appreciating in value as we speak and receive more words of gratitude. The world will be forever grateful.

Words of Wisdom
"I agree to give and receive thanks."

Let us be grateful to people who make us happy;
they are the charming gardeners who make our souls blossom.
—Marcel Proust

Gratitude unlocks the fullness of life.
It turns what we have into enough, and more.
It turns denial into acceptance, chaos to order,
confusion to clarity. It can turn a meal into a feast,
a house into a home, a stranger into a friend.
Gratitude makes sense of our past,
brings peace for today,
and creates a vision for tomorrow.
—Melody Beattie

It is up to us to give ourselves recognition.
If we wait for it to come from others,
we feel resentful when it doesn't,
and when it does, we may well reject it.
—Bernard Berkowitz

Feeling gratitude and not expressing it
is like wrapping a present and not giving it.
—William Arthur Ward

I would maintain that thanks are the highest form of thought,
and that gratitude is happiness doubled by wonder.
—Gilbert K. Chesterton

Make it a habit to tell people thank you.
To express your appreciation, sincerely and without
the expectation of anything in return. Truly appreciate life,
and you'll find that you have more of it.
—Ralph Marston[39]

You have it easily in your power to increase the sum total
of this world's happiness now. How? By giving a few words of
sincere appreciation to someone who is lonely or discouraged.
Perhaps you will forget tomorrow the kind words you say today,
but the recipient may cherish them over a lifetime.
—Dale Carnegie

Gratitude is something of which none of us can give too much.
For on the smiles, the thanks we give, our little gestures of
appreciation, our neighbors build their philosophy of life.
—A.J. Cronin

Appreciative words are the most powerful force for good on earth!
—George W. Crane

The deepest principle in human nature
is the craving to be appreciated.
—William James

One is taught by experience to put a premium on
those few people who can appreciate you for what you are.
—Gail Godwin

If the only prayer you ever say in your entire life
is "Thank you," it will be enough.
—Meister Eckhart

Focus on Today
I agree to give and receive thanks—TODAY!

Here are several steps you can take to enjoy saying "thank you" more often and receiving others' thanks more fully. Doing so, you can expect to have a better than average day! Record your thoughts in your journal.

1. What am I grateful for in this very moment?
   Example: Glenn offered to drive Michael to school so I could sleep in . . . Michael cleaned the kitchen without my reminding him . . . Michael remembered to give our dog his supplements . . . a potential business associate responded to my email positively . . . a friend was flexible about what time to meet for our walk together today (all this by 9 a.m.!) . . .

2. I'm going to pick three of the items above and actually speak my thanks to those involved within the next 24 hours. I'll also notice the results of speaking my thanks to these three people and record these in my journal.

3. Every time someone thanks me for something today, I will uncross my arms, look them in the eyes (if possible), smile, take a deep breath and say, "You're welcome," or, "My pleasure," and nothing else. I'll record in my journal how this felt.
   Example: Rita thanked me for helping her get satrted in the business. I felt glad to be of service.

   A friend thanked me for singing a special song for her. I felt embarrassed and said, "It's not really my key." She asked me to simply say, "Thank you," and receive her praise. (Ha!) I started again, looked at her, smiled and said "Thank you." I felt appreciative and appreciated.

I agree
to see the best
in myself and others.

The potential of the average person is like
a huge ocean unsailed, a new continent unexplored,
a world of possibilities waiting to be released and
channeled toward some great good.
—Brian Tracy[40]

Come with me, for a moment, on a journey back to your childhood; imagine yourself sitting at your desk in your elementary school classroom.

The teacher asks a question; the child next to you shoots her hand into the air and is called upon. She answers the question thoughtfully and beautifully, and after she's finished the entire class cheers at the top of their lungs. Everyone can tell what a wonderful answer it was.

The teacher smiles broadly and allows the hubbub to continue until it dies down naturally. All are eager for the next lesson. The teacher captivates everyone as she brings history to life in her dramatic re-telling. She asks how this story applies to something that's happened to you recently . . . and waits to see who will volunteer an answer.

Now it's your hand that shoots up into the air with confidence, and she calls on you expectantly. You share your thoughts on how the story shows that history repeats itself, and the class again explodes into applause, thrilling at the insight, pathos and power of your thoughts.

In the hallway after class, one of your classmates slaps you on the back and compliments you on your creative answer. Once again, you've been validated.

You are, in fact, being groomed for a lifetime of giving your best. Seeing the best in others comes naturally to you, as does supporting others to do the same. It has been taught, encouraged and rewarded for so long, it has simply become a way of life ....

Okay ... perhaps this is not how *your* normal school day was. But what if it had been, day after day, year after year? How would that have affected you? What abilities, skills and pathways in life would this kind of extraordinarily nurturing, supportive environment have opened up for you?

Here is the wonderful thing: *it's not too late.* We can create precisely that environment, today and every day. That's what this Agreement is all about.

In our family, we used to create a weekly theme in the form of a question to ponder each night at the dinner table. During "kindness week," we would ask (and answer): "Who was kind to me today?" and "Who was I kind to?" During "encouragement" week," we would ask, "Who encouraged me today—and whom did I encourage?" These questions gave us an opportunity to see the best in ourselves and others.

Barbara Marx Hubbard, my good friend and mentor, saw the best in me and helped me on the path to overcoming my tendency to be motivated by others' approval.

While working on a project together, Barbara said, "Marian, the only thing holding you back from making the greatest possible contribution to the world is your need for approval. When you're able to release that, you'll be able to achieve your heart's desire and be an unstoppable force for good in the world."

Barbara's seeing the best in me is what gave me the courage to let go of my long-held need for approval, opening the door to a more creative, positive life.

Nurture Your Best

To see the best in myself and others is to see ourselves created in God's image. Sometimes when I'm feeling stuck, I'll ask, "What would God do?" or, "What would Love do?"

As we enter this life, we are each endowed with innate wisdom, then given life experiences to learn to be fully who we are, to stretch to new limits and then break through them to experience new horizons, and to support one another to achieve even greater levels of excellence than we could have imagined alone.

To see the best in ourselves gives us the opportunity to raise our standards. What if we were to ask ourselves, "What small change could I make today that would shift one thing I do from average to excellent, from 'getting by' to being the best I can be?" This might be something meaningful but fairly easy to do.

One of my favorite motivational speakers, Jim Rohn, says the difference between successful and unsuccessful people is that successful people do those easy things that make a difference every day, while unsuccessful people find it just as easy *not* to do them.

Another life-changing teacher of mine is Tony Robbins. At the beginning of his "Personal Power" audio program, he asks us to choose something we commit to doing every day that will change our lives.[41]

When I first heard this I chose walking, and it has been a true gift for my life in the years since. It nurtures the best in me, giving me personal time with myself or uninterrupted time with my friends, connection to Nature, life-enhancing exercise for my body, and time to listen to audio programs that teach and inspire me further!

Can you imagine being surrounded by people who rejoice in being the best they can be?

What one easy step would give your life a new quality of excellence from this moment forward? What would nurture the best in you?

The Revolutionary Leader

Living this Agreement is the essence of what it means to be a Revolutionary leader: to foster an environment of genuine collaboration among people who see the best in each other.

In the 1970s, we often heard the phrase "leaderless" groups. This concept was borne of the effort to break off the shackles of authoritarian leadership and promote creativity and synergy.

But seeing the best in each other does not foster leaderless groups; on the contrary, it promotes leader*ful* groups—organizations, communities and households where every participant is encouraged to take the lead when he or she knows what to do next. The eyes take over when it's time to see and the ears tune in when it's time to hear. Each member has her function and naturally expresses her individual potential for the benefit of all. The group thus led is an organic entity— the organization as living organism. Barbara Marx Hubbard refers to this as "sapiential leadership."

Being a Revolutionary leader requires the skills of a mediator, not a courtroom lawyer; a facilitator and nurturer, not a dictator or a drill sergeant.

A Revolutionary leader is one who fosters an environment of genuine collaboration. This requires patience, compassion, humility and love. The result is the magic of synergy, where the power of one plus one is far greater than two.

Revolutionary leadership creates a new dynamic: the leader who doesn't have to know everything—nor pretend to.

David Neenan shares a story about a pivotal event in the evolution of his multi-million-dollar Neenan Company during a particularly challenging time in the company's history. At a boardroom meeting with the heads of his departments, realizing that he simply didn't know what to do to turn their circumstances around, he looked around the room and said, with utter candor, "I don't have the slightest idea what to do here." No one spoke. Then one brave soul said, "Well...why don't we work together? We've tried everything else."

Some might have called his admission a lack of leadership; I call it Revolutionary leadership. David says the company's future owed a great deal to this shift to collaborative leadership.

This is a vastly different scenario from a dog-eat-dog environment, with everyone doing his level best to scramble up the ladder to success while heedlessly stepping on anyone and everyone along the way! To be great, one does not need to be *better than.* The joy of being a Revolutionary leader is exhilarating.

What would it look like to see the best in everyone in your own workplace? To foster an environment of genuine collaboration? What simple steps can you take to foster an environment in which your teammates feel empowered to express their individual and collective potential?

This model of Revolutionary leadership is not for the workplace alone; it is equally practical—and equally powerful—in the home. Think of your home for a moment: is there one household member who lords it over the rest? What might it be like if all members of your household were allowed, even encouraged, to express themselves fully and take the lead naturally, creating a dance of leading, following, collaborating...leading, following, collaborating?

I see the best in you. I know that you can be a Revolutionary leader of the highest order. That you can excel in all that you do, with the grace that follows commitment and the joy that emanates from achievement.

I see the best in you. I see you enjoying the journey along the path of excellence, creativity and fulfillment.

I see the best in you. I hold you as fully capable of creating your own reality and making magnificent contributions to those in your life and your world.

I see the best in you.

Words of Wisdom
"I agree to see the best in myself and others."

Everyone has inside of him a piece of good news.
The good news is that you don't know how great you can be!
How much you can love! What you can accomplish!
And what your potential is!
—Anne Frank

The most common commodity
in this country is unrealized potential.
—Calvin Coolidge

Hide not your talents.
They for use were made.
What's a sundial in the shade?
—Benjamin Franklin

I know of no more encouraging fact than the unquestionable
ability of man to elevate his life by a conscious endeavor.
—Henry David Thoreau

One of the sanest, surest, and most generous joys of life
comes from being happy over the good fortune of others.
—Archibald Rutledge

If human beings are perceived as potentials rather than
problems, as possessing strengths instead of weaknesses,
as unlimited rather than dull and unresponsive,
then they thrive and grow to their capabilities.
—Robert Conklin

For some strange reason I can never be what I ought to be
until you are what you ought to be. And you can never be
what you ought to be until I am what I ought to be.
This is the way God's universe is made;
this is the way it is structured.
—Martin Luther King, Jr.

Next to excellence, comes the appreciation of it.
—William Makepeace Thackeray

I consider my ability to arouse enthusiasm among men
the greatest asset I possess. The way to develop the best
that is in a man is by appreciation and encouragement.
—Charles R. Schwab

My ability to throw a baseball was a gift—a God-given gift—
and I truly am appreciative of that gift. It took me a while
to figure that out and realize what a gift I had been given,
and when I finally did, I dedicated myself to be the best pitcher
that I possibly could be for as long as I possibly could.
—Nolan Ryan

Sometimes our light goes out
but is blown again into flame
by an encounter with another human being.
Each of us owes the deepest thanks to those
who have rekindled this inner light.
—Albert Schweitzer

Appreciation is a wonderful thing:
It makes what is excellent in others belong to us as well.
—Voltaire

Focus on Today
I agree to see the best in myself and others—TODAY!

Become a Revolutionary Leader by practicing this Agreement, starting today—and you'll be choosing a life of empowerment for yourself and for others. Record your thoughts in your journal.

1. What small change am I willing to make *today* that would shift one thing I do from average to excellent, from "getting by" to being the best I can be?

   Example: As a parent, I can make a commitment to engage our family in high-quality, interactive activities on nights the three of us have dinner together, rather than taking the lazy way out and letting us each do our own thing. This will improve the quality of our time spent and help deepen our connection with each other.

2. What simple steps can I take *today* that will empower my colleagues at work to be their very best?

   Example: Celebrate Glenn's successes—no matter how small—that result from the recent lead he has taken to support our growing business. Be sure to offer help and not criticize how he handles matters I may have handled differently. (Practice Agreement 6: Respect Our Differences!)

3. What simple steps can I take *today* that will empower others in my family to be their very best?

   Example: Remark to Michael about his phenomenal ability to achieve whatever he wants when he has the right attitude, makes the effort and uses "learning experiences" to improve his situation. Give him specific examples, such as his efforts to earn promotions in Civil Air Patrol.

AGREEMENT ELEVEN

I agree to look for blessings in disguise.

No matter how dark things seem to be or actually are, raise your sights and see possibilities— always see them, for they're always there.
—Norman Vincent Peale

Have you ever been really upset with something that happened to you, only to discover later that it actually changed your life for the better? If so, you know what it is to discover a blessing in disguise. This Agreement is easy to align with when everything is going well. When a seeming catastrophe befalls us, it's not so easy.

The Sun Behind the Cloud

When our son Michael was bitten by a Lyme-diseased tick in the summer of 2002, our world came to an abrupt halt. I don't think I had ever lost it as badly as I did during the months that followed.

I researched this debilitating disease day and night…joined the "Parents of Lyme Kids" Internet support group … hired and frequently spoke with four physicians from around the country ... monitored the voluminous medications and immune-enhancing supplements he ingested ... and even contracted for the building of a special frequency generator to aid in Michael's recovery.

Working to cope with Michael's acute illness kept me exceedingly busy, but my emotions would not stay contained. My anxiety ran rampant; I frequently broke down and wept with anguish, fear, frustration and exhaustion. Finally, I sought out spiritual and emotional help.

During a session with my counselor, David, I let it all out. I sobbed and screamed at the top of my lungs, "This is the worst nightmare a mother could have! Not even that her child would die, but that he would suffer terribly every day for the rest of his life!" David helped me to release my feelings that I was responsible for Michael's well-being, and that I was the only one who could help him find the way to recovery. He helped me to re-connect to the Source of Life, to know that Michael's path was his own and that all was in perfection in the grandest scheme.[42]

From this more peaceful place, I was able to start exploring other possibilities with Michael. Instead of asking, from the perspective of being a victim, "Why did this happen to us?" I began to wonder, What was the blessing in this disguise? How was this trial going to be of benefit to Michael? To me? Perhaps to all of humanity?

We don't know the answer to this yet, but I am convinced that for every cloud, there is a silver lining, and that the blessings hidden within this very large cloud must be very large and brilliant indeed.

I suggested to Michael, "Because you understand this disease, perhaps you'll be able to help another child recognize it sooner—and even help save his life." So many people are misdiagnosed with everything from multiple sclerosis to rheumatoid arthritis to chronic fatigue syndrome and fybromyalgia, only to discover years later that they are afflicted with Lyme disease—and that it has now gone so deep into every system of the body that it is far more complicated and difficult to treat.

And then, I suggested, there are Michael's experiences with the life-enhancing power of nutrition and the subtle energy of electromagnetics, which have taught him to expand his thinking beyond the usual Western medical practices to embrace the findings of other cultures and innovators. Perhaps Michael will become a doctor and help many people by integrating complementary techniques into his practices.

We don't know how Michael's bout with Lyme disease will serve him or others; we only know that it will.

How Will It Turn Out?

Think back to one of the worst incidents in your life. Can you find any good that came from it? With practice, you begin to identify all the positive outcomes that ultimately grow out of even seemingly horrendous circumstances. This tunes us up to be alert to such future possibilities, even while in the midst of calamity.

Looking back on my divorce, it would be easy to remember the pain and anguish. But going through this experience also helped me to get clear about what I *did* want in my life, possibly in a way that would not have otherwise occurred. On the day that I told my former husband of my decision to divorce, I told him precisely what I wanted in my life that I felt I could not have with him. Because my emotions were so intense and I was so clear about my choices for the future, I attracted that future to me. A year later I was with my future husband, with whom I have since fulfilled my heart's desire for more than 20 years.

Later, after giving birth to Michael at the age of 39, I spent three years feeling physically exhausted and often sick. At the time, I had not yet trained myself to ask this question in the midst of disappointment and difficulty, and I never had the thought, "I wonder what the silver lining is?" However, I would soon find the answer anyway.

As I sought desperately to regain my health and strength, a good friend introduced me to a line of nutrients that seemed to give my body just what it needed. Eight months later, my friend Gail and I decided to tell everyone we knew about these life-enhancing nutrients. We hung out our shingle—and for many ensuing years I enjoyed building a successful network marketing business, which I would never have considered if I hadn't needed help with my own health. The blessing goes way beyond a satisfying business to the depth of lifelong friendships developed through this work and the gift of early retirement as a reward for helping so many others.

Trust the Process

Sometimes, as in my years of post-natal malaise and the birth of our networking business, we are in a position to turn lemons into lemonade that we can clearly see and taste. It's great when that happens, when we can turn a lousy situation into a positive one. Often, though, it's not so easy to see or understand the outcome: we simply have to deal with the present conditions and, as my friend Joanne says, "trust the process."

In 2003, as he emerged in a weakened state from his struggles with Lyme disease, Michael re-entered the world of gymnastics that had been an integral part of his life since the age of two. Despite having missed four months of practice, he decided to begin competing. We were all thrilled to have him back in action, which blinded us to the fact that it was premature and dangerous. His lack of conditioning and confidence turned into a nightmare when he fell from the still rings, upside down, onto his head and neck.

He was paralyzed—not physically, but from his fear: he imagined he had broken his neck. His coach knew what we would later find out: "Michael will recover physically, but I'm concerned that he may never recover emotionally."

Only two years earlier, Michael had placed a close second in the state championships (by a twentieth of a point!), and had held aspirations to advance to the Olympics. But the coach was right: Michael has never fully returned to competitive gymnastics.

Seems pretty dismal, doesn't it? So what's the upside?

In the year after his last gymnastics competition, I asked Michael, "Was there anything good that came out of your not returning to gymnastics?" He immediately snapped, "No." I prodded him to consider it more carefully. He thought for a moment, then said, "Well, karate." He loves learning karate, and in the days when he was at the gym practicing his gymnastics four nights a week and competing on Saturdays, he'd had no time for any other sport.

"What else?" I asked. "Civil Air Patrol," he answered, now with a twinkle in his eye. "I *really* like Civil Air Patrol!" (It meets on Thursday nights, which had been a key gymnastics practice night.)

I pressed once more. "Can you think of anything else good that came out of that horrible fall? Any other blessings in disguise?" He thought for a moment, then smiled broadly and replied, "I have a lot more free time."

We think that's plenty for now.

At a deep level, we can know that everything is unfolding as it should, evolving as it will without our interference. If we look for the silver linings, the blessings in disguise, we will develop the habit of finding them. If we do this enough, we can even train ourselves so that when we are actually *in* one of those situations, we can find peace in the moment, rather than distress. We can learn to see through the disguise, and live in the blessing—in the light of the sun behind the cloud.

Words of Wisdom
"I agree to look for blessings in disguise."

Every exit is an entry somewhere else.
—Tom Stoppard

A stumbling block to the pessimist
is a stepping stone to the optimist.
—Eleanor Roosevelt

I am responsible. Although I may not be able to prevent
the worst from happening, I am responsible for my attitude
toward the inevitable misfortunes that darken life.
Bad things do happen; how I respond to them
defines my character and the quality of my life.
I can choose to sit in perpetual sadness, immobilized by the
gravity of my loss, or I can choose to rise from the pain
and treasure the most precious gift I have—life itself.
—Walter Anderson

I thank fate for having made me born poor.
Poverty taught me the true value of the gifts useful to life.
—Anatole France

God turns you from one feeling to another
and teaches by means of opposites,
so that you will have two wings to fly, not one.
—Mevlana Rumi

If you are distressed by anything external, the pain is
not due to the thing itself but to your own estimate of it;
and this you have the power to revoke at any moment.
—Marcus Aurelius

Let us learn to appreciate there will be times
when the trees will be bare, and look forward to the time
when we may pick the fruit.
—Anton Chekhov[43]

I thank Thee, first, because I was never robbed before;
second, because although they took my purse they
did not take my life; third, because although they took my all,
it was not much; and fourth because it was I who was robbed,
and not I who robbed.
—Matthew Henry

Both abundance and lack exist simultaneously in our lives,
as parallel realities. It is always our conscious choice which
secret garden we will tend...when we choose not to focus on what
is missing from our lives but are grateful for the abundance
that's present—love, health, family, friends, work, the joys of
nature and personal pursuits that bring us pleasure—the
wasteland of illusion falls away and we experience Heaven on
earth.
—Sarah Ban Breathnach

Some folks go through life pleased that the glass is half full.
Others spend a lifetime lamenting that it's half-empty.
The truth is: There is a glass with a certain volume of liquid in it.
From there, it's up to you!
—Dr. James S. Vuocolo[44]

Focus on Today
I agree to look for blessings in disguise—TODAY!

Practice identifying possible positive outcomes of seemingly negative occurrences in your life. This will give you practice transforming times of struggle into realizing blessings in your life. Record your thoughts in your journal.

1. What were some seemingly negative happenings from my past and blessings associated with those events?

    Example: My father died. BLESSING: Once my mom was unburdened of her role as caregiver, I got to really know her for the first time.

    Example: My two-year consulting contract ended and I'd done no marketing to find my next contract. I was without work. BLESSING: I was now free to respond to a friend's plea for help on a project that turned into my next vocation, making what I felt was a significant contribution.

2. What are some of my negative thoughts about current circumstances in my life? Using my imagination, what are some possible blessings in disguise corresponding to each of these negative thoughts?

    Example: I hate commuter traffic! BLESSING: Tomorrow I can use this precious time to listen to that parenting audiotape, which gives me valuable tips for communicating with my teenager.

    Example: This project is impossible—why did I get stuck with it? BLESSING: The only way to complete it is to learn some new skills—skills I may be able to apply later and for which I may even be paid more!

AGREEMENT TWELVE

I agree to lighten up!

Once you can accept the universe as
matter expanding into nothing that is something,
wearing stripes with plaid comes easy.
—Albert Einstein

My father, who was one of my favorite teachers, used to say, "Who's responsible for you having a good time at the party?" *I am*, came the answer that I learned from an early age; *only me*. Not the host or hostess, not the music or the guests, not the food or the games. No matter what's going on, I am the only one who has the power to make me enjoy myself (or not).

Our whole life is like one big party—and my father's rule applies here, too.

If you're waiting for your significant other to create joy in your relationship, give it up.

If you're waiting for things to get better at work so you can enjoy your job more, give it up.

Indeed, if you're waiting for *anything* to happen or change or improve before you can start to enjoy your life, *give it up!*

It's time for a Revolution!

Remember how we opened our discussion of the very first Agreement? "Some day, when I have the time ...."?

If you notice yourself heaving a heavy sigh and thinking, "When the kids go off to college ..." "When I get my raise ..." "When we move ..." "When I get married ..." "When I get my braces off ..."—give it up, let it go, free yourself from the "*Some day ...*" trap.

This may be the last Agreement, but there's no reason you can't implement it first, immediately, right now, this very minute! Make a declaration: *No more "Some day ..."!*

Stop waiting and live a positive life. Stop waiting and *give* to life. Become a Revolutionary: show the world how to create joy in every moment.

And en*joy* the moment—every moment. After all, the moment is going to be here, no matter what; would you rather suffer through it, or enjoy it? It's nothing but a choice, and it's a choice that could change your life. A choice that could change your world.

Buckminster Fuller offered, "God ... is a verb not a noun ... is loving, not the abstraction of love."[45] When you are love in action, your light illuminates the way for those ready to join you in this revolution.

Lighten Up! Smile. Laugh. Love. It's good for your health. And mine!

A Reverse Epiphany

One day in 1995, as I disembarked from a plane in Miami after an unusually bumpy flight, I had a sort of reverse epiphany: all of a sudden, circumstances seemed just as far from *light* as they could be.

I was still on edge from the rough flight. The airport was jammed; the heat was sweltering; people were exhaling nicotine and tar at me; the smog was thick; people all around me were complaining loudly and grumpily; and to top it all off, my ride was late. Everything about my situation felt heavy, dark, glum, and in every way the *opposite* of "light."

It was a moment of endarkenment!

I forced myself to direct my own pontification at myself, and thought, "There's always something to enjoy about the moment ..."—and I began to laugh out loud, because I could not find *one single thing* to enjoy about this moment—not one! All at once the absurdity of the situation struck me, and made me laugh even more: *I was enjoying the fact that I couldn't find a single thing to enjoy!*

"So why not laugh at the absurdity of life?" I asked myself. "Why not smile at a stranger?" And so I did.

I am inspired by my friend Vivian's life purpose: "To make a positive difference in the life of everyone I meet."

When I go about my day with this thought in mind, I am amazed at the difference in my interactions; how often I smile at someone; the joy I feel; the peacefulness I feel about others.

I hope you'll join me in doing this for just one hour—and then choose to extend that hour to the rest of your life!

Discovering Now

In 2000, I lost my joy. I went looking for it everywhere: in my relationship with my husband; in satisfaction stemming from my work; in my connection with God. I spent hours and hours in the mountains every week, hoping that through my connection with Nature I would find the answer.

I asked, "What am I to do next? Please show me the way! There must be more to life than this. I am almost 50 years old and I have not yet saved the world. I know I'm here for a greater purpose, and I am ready to *get on* with it! What should I do?!"

No answers came. At least, not the ones I wanted to hear.

All I heard was: "It's not what you do, it's how you do it. Do whatever you like." Well, I didn't *know* what I liked!

I searched all year. I read personal growth books and attended course after course, seeking the answer. And then, *bingo!* I found it. It was something I had already known, but only intellectually. Suddenly it became as real to me as my skin.

Be here now. Simple ... right?

Be here now. "What do you mean," I asked the still, small voice inside me, "where else would I be?" But that one was easy: I would be somewhere *else*. Or more accurately, some *when* else: my mind was often away from *now*, mulling over some past event or worrying obsessively over some imagined future. I looked like I was here, all the lights were on, the car was in the driveway ... but my mind had snuck away to fret.

Be here now. All at once I got it—and my negative emotions vanished. They had to: they simply could not survive the *now*, because they all seemed to be related to something that happened in a remembered past or an imagined future ... but they weren't real any longer. In fact, they never really had been.

There was only, always, *now*.

When I first moved to Colorado years ago, my friend Trish would call me from DC with worry in her voice. "How are you doing, Marian? Are you doing okay financially?" My favorite answer was, "If you took a snapshot of me at any moment in time, my life would look great." That was my way of saying that it *looked* like I had a great life ... but I was really worried about the future, or still appalled about what had happened to me yesterday.

My upbringing in the Jewish tradition of suffering had its impact on me. Even now, I will ask my aunt, "How are you?" and she will wince as she replies with an elongated sigh, "Okay ..."— even if she's having the best day of her life. We are taught to suffer, to remember the atrocities that befell our people. Our mothers, aunts and grandmothers modeled how to be martyrs, to sacrifice personal desire for the good of the family. "I'll take the shriveled up piece of meat. Here, you have the tender one." It was rare to find an adult in our family (especially a matriarch) who expressed feeling really good, happy and content. I had no models to show me how to lighten up!

When I finally made the shift to *now*, to no yesterday or tomorrow, the drama and suffering were gone and an ease set in.

I learned that I could create joy in my relationships, my work and my life, simply by being present. By living "in the moment." And it is *good*. In the stillness of every moment, I find peace. Joy. Bliss. Ecstasy. Love beyond the ability of any words to fully convey.

On the outside, my life looks the same. I have not chosen to change my work, my relationships, my home state, my hair color, my name, nor anything else visible. But my life is *filled* with joyful moments.

I have a new primary aim in life: "To fully enjoy life and experience love in every moment." It keeps me on track—and it attracts people to my work and my life who also choose to enjoy their lives. What a blessing to work with positive people!

Would you rather be surrounded by people who are loving, positive people enjoying their lives? Or by people who are suffering? (Remember, like attracts like; misery loves company!) What's your choice? I hope it is to join me as a Revolutionary leader. To be the light that you truly are. To exude the joy that is your birthright. To laugh unabashedly and bring laughter to others. To create joy in your relationships, your work and your life.

Lighten Up! In so doing, you light up the world!

Words of Wisdom
"I agree to lighten up!"

I try to learn from the past, but I plan for the future
by focusing exclusively on the present.
That's where the fun is.
—Donald Trump

My mission is to make a positive difference
in the lives of everyone I meet.
—Vivian Sacucci

If it's true that we are here to help others,
then what exactly are the others here for?
—author unknown

Life loves to be taken by the lapel and told:
"I'm with you kid. Let's go."
—Maya Angelou

If we don't make some changes,
the status quo will remain the same.
—author unknown

Change is inevitable,
except from a vending machine.
—Robert C. Gallagher

Despite the cost of living,
have you noticed how it remains so popular?
—author unknown

God put me on earth to accomplish
a certain number of things.
Right now I am so far behind,
I will live forever.
—author unknown

It may be that your sole purpose in life
is simply to serve as a warning to others.
—Ruth E. Renkel[46]

Experience is something you don't get
until just after you need it.
—Sir Laurence Olivier

If you try to succeed, and fail,
what have you done?
Stephen Wright

And forget not that the earth delights to feel your bare feet
and the winds long to play with your hair.
Kahlil Gibran

I plan on living forever. So far, so good.
—author unknown

i thank You God for most this amazing
day; for the leaping greenly spirits of trees,
and a blue true dream of sky; and for everything
which is natural which is infinite which is yes.
—e.e. cummings

Focus on Today
I agree to lighten up—TODAY!

The first agreement ("I agree to live my mission") encouraged you to identify what you love to do—and then to live it. We've come full circle: with this agreement, you commit to live your life in joy. Record your thoughts in your journal.

1. Review my mission statement from Agreement One. Re-write it (or change it, if appropriate) and add the words "enjoy," "joy" or "joyfully" if they are not already in it:

   Example: I joyfully commit to being a devoted wife, mother and friend who wants to bless family, friends and people I meet with the gift of growing older with grace, hope and financial help. (I got this wonderful statement from my business associate, Teri Morelli.)

2. What one small thing can I do *today* to lighten up my life?

   Example: Have fun raising my teenage son by consciously using more humor and a less lecturing tone of voice.

3. What has happened as a result of doing that one small thing?

$\mathcal{I}$ CHOOSE...

Some believe there is nothing one man or one woman can do against the enormous array of the world's ills—against misery, against ignorance, or injustice and violence. Yet many of the world's great movements, of thought and action, have flowed from the work of a single person. ...A young woman reclaimed the territory of France ...32-year-old Thomas Jefferson proclaimed that all men are created equal. "Give me a place to stand," said Archimedes, "and I will move the world." These [people] moved the world, and so can we all.
—Robert F. Kennedy

The future is now: you are creating it in this very moment. What do you choose?

I choose to surround myself with like-minded, like-hearted (and *light*-hearted!) friends. To surround myself with:

People who are passionate about living their missions and who support one another to achieve their goals and dreams;

People I can trust to always speak their truth, with compassion for themselves and others;

People who look within themselves for clues to learning and transformation when emotions flare;

People who are open to continuously choosing and re-choosing what works and allowing themselves to change what doesn't;

People who listen with their hearts rather than imposing their own interpretations on what others say;

People who understand that true collaboration within a rich diversity is what brings out the best in each of us;

People I can trust to always take problems directly to the source (especially if it's me!), and who will remind me to do the same;

People who respect my right to my own perspective and who honor our diverse choices;

People who acknowledge me for the contributions I make and graciously accept my acknowledgment of them;

People who strive for excellence and who see the best in themselves and others, who constantly expect the best from our circumstances and appreciate the blessings even before they may be obvious;

People with whom I can effortlessly lighten up and feel completely free!

... to surround myself, in other words, with people who embrace the principles behind these Revolutionary Agreements as a guide to creating a positive life.

I invite you to join me!

CREATING A POSITIVE WORLD

"This all sounds good and makes so much sense to me as I read it . . . but how do I keep it alive, as a real ongoing experience in my everyday life? Not just today and tomorrow, but next week, next month, next year?"

One answer, of course, is to do what we always do with books that hold special meaning for us: highlight passages we want to remember, make notes in the margins, read and re-read. Reading through one Agreement just before sleep, or first thing in the morning upon awakening, is a great way to imprint the material more deeply in your consciousness.

Consider repeating each "Focus on Today" exercise at the end of each chapter every day for 30 days (that's one per month for a year), or until each Agreement has become so intrinsically a part of you that their daily practice comes naturally, effortlessly and with joy.

To deepen your experience of these Agreements (and begin to transform your world as a result), you can become part of a support network that nurtures these ideas as a tangible reality in your everyday lives together. This is exactly what Glenn and I did in 1985 with about a dozen friends and colleagues when we co-created the Geneva Group. This forum for like-minded, like-hearted souls continues to this day to support its mission:

To develop and maximize our personal growth and evolution, thus enhancing our relationships and all life on the planet through reflecting unconditional love, support, and well-being.

Connect with a worldwide community of people who are using these Agreements and who are committed to co-creating a positive future at www.RevolutionaryAgreements.com.

To start your own group, simply share this book with a few friends, people you care about. Ask them if they'd like to start a study group around the Revolutionary Agreements. Choose a time when you can gather uninterrupted. One very practical way to use this time together is to devote each session to discussing and sharing your experiences with a single Agreement.

Guidelines for Community Gatherings

When you meet, use the first few minutes of your session very simply to come together and establish your sense of being present with one another. When the Geneva Group meets, we sometimes start out with uplifting music and take a few minutes to connect with each other, mostly without speaking. It's amazing how much more deeply we can connect when we're not talking (and this certainly precludes any chance of "letting the words get in the way"!). Some reach out to touch another's hand; others embrace their friends with a hug, still others share a smile and a soft "Hello." Mostly we simply reconnect by witnessing the joy in each others' eyes, which are truly the windows to the soul.

You will find your own way to connect. If you're not quite comfortable with or ready for the intimacy of silent greetings, you might start with a simple checking-in process. Sitting in a circle, ask each person to complete this phrase however he or she likes: "What I feel like saying is ..." Each person in turn completes this phrase to let everyone else know how they're doing in just a few words, and to help release any thoughts that might keep them from being completely present with the group. Continue this around the circle as many times as is necessary for each person to feel ready to participate fully. At any point, anyone can conclude their own check-in by simply saying, "I'm present." When everyone has said, "I'm present," you're ready to move on.

However you elect to begin, it's a good idea to *identify a specific process* and not just "wing it." Rituals help us connect with each other and ground us in the essence of this work. Opening with a silent greeting or with a verbal check-in are rituals; a short meditation or prayer can be a ritual: "God, please guide us to know the depth of the meaning behind the words of these Agreements, that we may be uplifted and may uplift others."

From this place of quieted mind, one person reads your group's mission, if you have one. For example, "Our mission is to support each other in effectively using the Revolutionary Agreements to live positive lives and to co-create a positive future for all." Each person in turn then reads one of the Agreements, until all twelve have been read aloud.

Explore the Agreement you've chosen for that gathering. Each is multi-faceted like a sparkling diamond, a reflection of who you are and who you choose to become. Let yourself fully explore the potential of living this Agreement. Allow yourself to go to places in your mind and heart where you may not have traveled before.

Share your experiences implementing these Agreements at home, at work and in your world. Be good listeners for each other, allowing each person to be fully heard. Problem-solve only if requested by the speaker.

Encourage each member of the group to facilitate a regularly scheduled gathering, so that all participate and no one is burdened. The greater the participation, the greater the reward. For more facilitation tips, consult *The Co-Creator's Handbook*.[47]

Revolutionary Agreements in the Workplace

You may want to introduce these Agreements in other spheres of influence in your life, both to share them with others and to make your life more supportive for you as well. Your family, neighborhood group, congregation, and any number of other groups in your life may be appropriate and fruitful places to do this.

For many of us, the place that makes the most immediate sense is our place of work.

Many work teams have used these Agreements as a basis for supporting their organizations' missions and enhancing communication skills. Some have used them as the foundation for comprehensive training programs; others simply read each Agreement aloud in turn at the beginning of each staff meeting to help align the team and set the tone for honest communications. Some have progressed through the Agreements by choosing one to focus attention on for one week or one month, then moving on to each of the others in turn.

The potential impact of these Agreements in the place where we spend most of our lives—our place of work—is huge. Imagine the positive changes that would occur if your peers, supervisors and staff followed the principles of Truth, Acceptance and Gratitude that lie at the heart of the Revolutionary Agreements!

Transforming the World

In *The Tipping Point: How Little Things Can Make a Big Difference*, Malcolm Gladwell explains how small groups of influential individuals play a critical role in creating mass consciousness. "It's easier to remember and appreciate something, after all, if you discuss it for two hours with your best friends. . . . Small, close-knit groups have the power to magnify the epidemic potential of a message or idea."[48]

As Revolutionary leaders, we have just such a "message

with epidemic potential." We choose to promote a new way of thinking, to live positive lives, to dare to think and act in such a way that we change a world of fear and contraction to one of love and expansion.

As a Revolutionary, my personal mission is *to foster an environment of genuine collaboration in which we can all achieve our individual and collective potential.*

It is clear to me that a sweeping, world-wide change, from a fear-based to a love-based existence, is only an evolutionary step away. We can make the choice to join together and speed up this natural next phase of our development by adopting these Agreements as our way of life—and in so doing, move into the fullness of our potential as loving beings, each fueled by a Divine spark of life.

Why not nurture the true nature within each of us—the innocence, joy and unconditional love of the child we once were—and bring it to fullness? In so doing, we may avert the further destruction and degradation of our world as brought about by the prevailing mass fear-based consciousness.

My deepest desire is that you'll join me in this Revolution by helping me to create a tidal wave of powerful, positive and enduring impact on our world. If this sounds ambitious, remember this: throughout history, it is individuals, caught up in the impassioned grip of an idea whose time has come, who have always created the most lasting, positive impact.

As Margaret Mead put it so beautifully in her most famously quoted statement, "Never doubt that a small group of thoughtful, committed people can change the world. Indeed, it is the only thing that ever has."[49]

Simply follow this guide to living a positive life of Truth, Acceptance and Gratitude, and you will achieve what Gandhi suggested: *Be the change you wish to see in the world.*

SHARE YOUR STORIES

I invite you to tell your stories so that others may learn from your experiences and feel the common bond of those committed to "being the change we wish to see in the world."

How's the Revolution going in your life? At your place of work? In your home? In your community?

This book is only a beginning. Future books in the Revolutionary Agreements series will focus on applying the Agreements in the work place, in the home, in our marriages, as parents and as teammates, and will present the experiences of readers just like you.

Visit us at www.RevolutionaryAgreements.com, and share your stories!

$\mathcal{N}$OTES

Birth of the Revolutionary Agreements

1 The personal development program that inspired the Geneva Group Agreements, which later evolved into the Revolutionary Agreements, is "Money and You: Management by Agreement." I am grateful to Marshall Thurber for his brilliant design and expert facilitation of this program, which was life-changing for me. Thurber was also founder of the enormously successful Hawthorne/Stone Real Estate Company of San Francisco, written about in *New Realities* magazine (Brown 1977). According to Laurie Weiss, in *What is the Emperor Wearing? Truth-Telling in Business Relationships*, "The Hawthorne/Stone agreements are reputed to have been created as 'rules of the game' in a business that was introducing the radical (in the mid-1970s) concept of using principles of the heart in a business environment. The agreements were said to be ideas that were tested by the working group to see what impact they would have on the productivity and personal growth of the people involved. Those principles that had a positive effect were retained; the others were discarded." My special thanks to Laurie Weiss and her husband Jon for producing the "Money and You" program in Colorado. For information on current programs based on "Money and You," go to www.excellerated.com and www.businessandu.com.

2 Named the Geneva Group, this forum was founded June 8, 1985, at the home of Glenn and Marian Head and Gail Hoag, in Geneva Park, Boulder, Colorado. We owe a debt of gratitude to the founding members (in addition to Glenn, Gail and myself): Lycia Adams, Don Darling, Thomas Duncan, John Erhard, Dale and Dar Emme, Sigrid Farwell, Susan O'Neill,

Sharon Proudfit, Lindsay Robinson, Donne Ruiz, Diane Schmitz, Liz Gardener and Carol Ann Wilson Fullmer. We are deeply grateful to Carol Hoskins for keeping the forum alive and well during my parenting years; also Laurie and Jon Weiss and others who remain the core of this evolving forum that continues to meet monthly and is guided by its mission: "To develop and maximize our personal growth and evolution thus enhancing our relationships and all life on the planet through reflecting unconditional love, support, growth and well-being."

3   The Soviet-American Citizens' Summits mentioned here and discussed throughout this book were created and produced by Rama Joyti Vernon and Barbara Marx Hubbard, alongside their Soviet counterparts from the Soviet Peace Committee and other state-authorized agencies. Rama is Founding President of the Center for International Dialogue, Founder and President Emeritus of Women of Vision and Action (WOVA), co-founder of the *Yoga Journal* and citizen-diplomat for conflict resolution dialogues worldwide. Mikhail Gorbachev credited her citizen diplomacy efforts as a major contribution to ending cold war stereotypes.

Barbara Marx Hubbard is President of the Foundation for Conscious Evolution, founding member of the World Future Society and an internationally recognized author and lecturer. She is mentioned lovingly throughout this book as one of the author's friends and mentors, and her important work is footnoted further in Note 41.

An inspiring and informative book documented the vision and results of the first Summit: *Citizen Diplomacy Progress Report 1989: The USSR*, edited by Sandy McCune Jeffrey (now Sandy Westin) (Boulder: Clearinghouse for Citizen Diplomacy, 1989). In addition to documentation of the hundreds of projects jointly initiated during that first auspicious convening in Washington DC, essays on citizen diplomacy by Rama Vernon, Barbara Marx Hubbard, members of the Soviet Peace Committee and others shine the light on this epochal moment in history.

Following is an excerpt from pages 46–47, reprinted with permission of the editor, which was written by Summit collaborator Andre Nuikin, then Senior Researcher in the Institute of Arts Studies of the USSR Ministry of Culture:

"It is impossible to approach this diplomacy with old yard-sticks, demanding perceptible results, well-planned stages, constructive forms. This is not a mechanical increase of uniting structures that is taking place here, but an alchemy of souls, the sacrament of the birth of a living being from the effect of Aladdin's lamp. The main argument in this diplomacy is not the number of warheads, not the productivity of blast furnaces, nor the figures of commodity circulation, but the expression in the eyes of people who meet one another, the strength of hand-shakes, goodwill and the wit of jokes. Therefore we must meet, talk, touch one another, and smile, although for political and scientific generalizations, all this material is purely ephemeral and beyond all calculation.

" 'Beauty will save the world!' proclaimed Fyodor Dostoyevsky. Indeed, it is precisely beauty that will save the world. Not museum beauty, of course, but that which looks for an outlet (but so far finds it so rarely) in our souls. No, not just any kind of beauty will save us; the flight of a missile with nuclear warheads too may be seen as beautiful. Our salvation is in the beauty of human relations—generosity, conscience, friendliness, trust and high intellect. By 'high' I mean the intellect which is not separated from the beauty of spiritual movements, does not contradict them but is blended with them indissolubly. Here we also have to revise the yardsticks and standards.

"Spirituality today is, I would say, sympathy for the world which has attained a scope of all mankind. To be spiritual means to have an open heart for all global problems of the century, to take to heart all troubles of one's people and mankind, to re-joice at their joys, to be personally responsible for the past, the present, and the future."

Unfortunately, *Citizen Diplomacy* is out of print; for reprints of selected sections, contact the editor: Sandy Westin, PO Box 67, Pisgah Forest, NC 28768.

4 In October 1985, ten spiritual leaders (two each from five ma-jor religions) and eight elected officials from parliaments on

five continents met in Tarrytown, New York to explore the possibility of a dialogue intermingling their perspectives. As a result, the Global Forum of Spiritual and Parliamentary Leaders on Human Survival was birthed. Alongside our colleagues from Global Family, a UN Non-Governmental Organization (NGO), Glenn and I were honored to collaborate on the design and implementation of the first Global Forums. In April 1988, under the coordination of Akio Matsumura, a Global Survival Conference brought nearly 200 spiritual and legislative leaders to the historic university city of Oxford, England. For five days, parliamentarians and cabinet members met with cardinals, swamis, bishops, rabbis, imams, monks and elders. Among them were the Dalai Lama, Mother Teresa, the Archbishop of Canterbury, Cardinal Koenig of Vienna, and Native American spiritual leader Chief Oren Lyons. These leaders conferred with experts on the issues, including astronomer Carl Sagan, Soviet scientist Evguenij Velikhov, Gaia scientist James Lovelock, Kenyan environmental leader Wangari Maathai, and Cosmonaut Valentina Tereshkova.

In the end, the vision a few had worked for became a shared vision among many. Spiritual and parliamentary leaders from 52 countries, along with participating scientists and influential journalists, left Oxford agreeing that "we both need and desire to work together" to protect Earth and all that lives on it. Future Forums in Moscow, Rio de Janeiro and Kyoto served to solidify relationships and strategies for implementation.

5   Head, Marian and Glenn. *The American Team: 7 Steps to Genuine Teamwork in the White House and Beyond.* Boulder: New World Design Center, 1992. Prepared and submitted by invitation to the Clinton/Gore Presidential transition team, and subsequently incorporated into *Blueprint for Presidential Transition*, Washington DC, 1992.

6   Anderson, Carolyn, Barbara Marx Hubbard, and Marian Head. *Rings of Empowerment.* San Francisco: Global Family, 1993.

7   Weiss, Laurie. *What Is the Emperor Wearing? Truth-Telling in Business Relationships.* Boston: Butterworth-Heinemann, 1998.

8   Brook, Brian. *Love Styles: Re-Engineering Marriage for the New Millennium.* Denver: ProSe, 2000.

9   Anderson, Carolyn and Katharine Roske. *The Co-Creator's Handbook: An Experiential Guide for Discovering Your Life's Purpose and Building a Co-Creative Society.* San Francisco: Global Family, 2001.

The One Agreement

10 In *Essential Spirituality: The 7 Central Practices to Awaken Heart and Mind* (New York: John Wiley & Sons, 1999), Roger Walsh, M.D., Ph.D., beautifully summarizes the essential message of the seven great world religions: Judaism: *He is in all, and all is in Him.* Christianity: *The Kingdom of Heaven is within you.* Islam: *Those who know themselves know their Lord.* Confucianism: *Those who know completely their own nature, know heaven.* Chinese Book of Changes: *In the depth of the soul, one sees the Divine, the One.* Hinduism: *Individual consciousness and universal consciousness are one.* Buddhism: *Look within, you are the Buddha.*

11 Ruiz, don Miguel. *The Four Agreements: A Practical Guide to Personal Freedom.* San Rafael, CA: Amber-Allen Publishing, 1997.

12 All quotations within this book have either been verified by the online versions of *Bartlett's Familiar Quotations, Simpson's Contemporary Quotations* or *Columbia World of Quotations*; or have been considered by the author to be widely attributed to the named source if found on at least five different quotation web sites, unless indicated otherwise in these Notes.

Agreement One

13 Myss, Caroline. *Sacred Contract: Awakening Your Divine Potential.* Three Rivers, MI: 3 Rivers Press, 2003.

14 Anderson and Roske. *The Co-Creator's Handbook* (Ibid).

15 Bronson, Po. *What Should I Do With My Life? The True Story of People Who Answered the Ultimate Question.* New York: Random House, 2003.

16 Covey, Stephen. *The 7 Habits of Highly Successful People: Powerful Lessons in Personal Change*. New York: Simon & Schuster, 1990.

17 Covey, Stephen, A. Roger Merrill and Rebecca R. Merrill. *First Things First: To Live, To Love, To Learn, To Leave a Legacy*. New York: Fireside, 1996).

18 Gerber, Michael. *The E-Myth Revisited: Why Most Small Businesses Don't Work and What to Do About It*. New York: HarperBusiness, 1995. 190–209.

19 Blanchard, Kenneth and Spencer Johnson. *The One-Minute Manager.* New York: Berkely Pub Group, 1983.

Agreement Two
20 The team of astronauts aboard the spaceship Columbia were described by Gary Dorsey in the *Baltimore Sun*, February 7, 2003.

Agreement Three
21 Ruiz, *The Four Agreements: A Practical Guide to Personal Freedom* (Ibid).

22 Inscription on the Oracle of Apollo at Delphi, Greece, 6th century B.C. The words are traditionally ascribed to the "Seven Sages" or "Seven Wise Men" of ancient Greece, and specifically to Solon of Athens (c. 640–c. 558 B.C.).

Agreement Four
23 Johnson, Spencer. *Who Moved My Cheese? An Amazing Way to Deal With Change in Your Work and Life*. New York, Putnam Publishing Group, 1998.

24 See McCamant, Kathryn, *Cohousing: A Contemporary Approach to Housing Ourselves*, 2nd Edition, Berkeley: Ten Speed Press, 1993. This book and its author guided us and many thousands of others on our community-building journey.

25 Johnson, *Who Moved My Cheese?* (Ibid).

Agreement Five

26 Wiesel, Elie. "Have You Learned The Most Important Lesson Of All?" *Parade 24 May, 1992.*

27 Since the original writing of this book, I have discovered *Parenting With Love and Logic: Teaching Children Responsibility*, by Foster Cline, M.D. and Jim Fay (Colorado Springs: Pinon Press, 1990). This is a magnificent program (books, audiotapes, seminars and more) on how to interact with your children and teens in an empowering way that minimizes stress and maximizes cooperation (www.loveandlogic.com). I only wish I had learned these tools before Michael became a teenager—but it's never too late!

28 I have learned a great deal about myself and the filters through which I listen from Carol McCall's "Empowerment of Listening" seminars. McCall is founder of the Institute for Global Listening and Communication (www.listeningprofitsu.com) and author of *Listen! There's a World Waiting To Be Heard* (New York: Vantage Press, 2000).

29 Quoted in *Publishers Weekly*.

30 As listed in the February 2001 Featured Quotes of the International Listening Association (www.listen.org/quotations/quotes_feb2001.html).

Agreement Seven

31 For a fuller description of how two monogamous couples shared a home together for nearly 13 years, read Brook's *Love Styles* (Ibid).

Agreement Eight

32 *Fortune 6 Jun, 1988*: 50.

33 Covey, *The 7 Habits of Highly Effective People* (Ibid): 90.

34 "The Samurai." *The Highlander.* Third season episode. As spoken by Midori Koto.

35 Paraphrased by Terry Bragg, author of *31 Days to High Self-Esteem* (Salt Lake City: Peacemakers Training, 1997). The passage that was likely the inspiration for this quotation came from Fuller's book *Critical Path* (New York: St. Martin's Press, 1981), pp. 262–263: "Humans are designed to learn how to survive only through trial-and-error-won knowledge," or from pp. 229–230: "Class-one evolution accounts for humans' presence on Earth. It accounts for their having always been born naked, helpless for months, and inexperienced—ergo, ignorant, hungry, thirsty, curious, and therefore fated to learn how to survive only through trial-and-error-won, progressive accumulation of experience."

36 Reprinted by permission from Tom Peters (www.tompeters.com).

Agreement Nine

37 This oft-quoted passage appears to be expanded from the following, which appeared in an interview in a 1989 edition of *Time* magazine: "The hunger for love is much more difficult to remove than the hunger for bread."

38 On CBS TV, December 30, 1957. The full quotation is: "No matter how big a nation is, it is not stronger than its weakest people, and as long as you keep a person down, some part of you has to be down there to hold him down, so it means that you cannot soar as you might otherwise."

39 Reprinted by permission from Ralph Marston (www.DailyMotivator.com).

Agreement Ten

40 Reprinted by permission from Brian Tracy (www.briantracy.com, 858-481-2977).

41 Robbins, Anthony. *Personal Power II.* www.personalpower.com.

Agreement Eleven

42 I met David Kimmel in an exceptional spiritual development program developed by Arjuna Ardagh of the Living Essence Foundation. David was one of the program's facilitators; he helped me personally through several deep issues that took a lifetime to accumulate and days to dissolve. Years later, when faced with mounting uncontrollable emotions around my son's illness, I thought of Arjuna's process and David's ability to help me relax into the vast love of God. Although this time we worked long distance by phone, David proved once again to be an exceptional spiritual counselor. David can be contacted by email at dkimmel@sbcglobal.net.

43 Quoted in www.studyworld.com and www.brainyquote.com.

44 Reprinted by permission from Dr. James Vuocolo (www.life-coachconsulting.com).

Agreement Twelve

45 Fuller, R. Buckminster. *No More Secondhand God*. Carbondale, IL: Southern Illinois University, 1963.

46 Attributed to Renkel at http://dqs.worldatwar.org/robots/430.html.

Creating A Positive World

47 Anderson and Roske. *The Co-Creator's Handbook* (Ibid) is a source book for Global Family core groups in 40 countries around the world. Serving thousands who choose to co-create a positive future for our world by shifting consciousness from fear and separation to love and unity, Global Family promotes activities and processes that enable people to experience deeper connections to each other, to the earth and to their Source. *The Co-Creator's Handbook* includes Co-Creator's Agreements, an early version of the Revolutionary Agreements (www.globalfamily.net).

48 Gladwell, Malcolm. *The Tipping Point: How Little Things Can Make a Big Difference*. New York: Little Brown and Company, 2000.

49 The Institute for Intercultural Studies in New York, founded by Margaret Mead in 1944, explains on their web page, www.mead2001.org: "Although the Institute has received many inquiries about this famous admonition by Margaret Mead, we have been unable to locate when and where it was first cited, becoming a motto for many organizations and movements. We believe it probably came into circulation through a newspaper report of something said spontaneously and informally. We know, however, that it was firmly rooted in her professional work and that it reflected a conviction that she expressed often, in different contexts and phrasings."

$\mathcal{A}$BOUT THE AUTHOR

Marian Head has been initiating revolutions in business, government and education since the early 1970s.

Her diverse experiences as organizer, facilitator, entrepreneur and leader have ranged from being President of her 4-H Club as a child; to serving the US Senate (which she calls "the agreement capitol of the world") as its first Manager for Educational Development; to initiating and co-chairing the Boulder Graduate School's Department of Organizational Transformation and Change; to being program coordinator for the Soviet-American Citizens' Summits in Washington DC and Moscow and co-facilitating the Global Forum of Spiritual and Parliamentary Leaders in Oxford and Moscow.

In 1985 Marian co-founded the Geneva Group, a network of businesspeople formed around a set of principles that has since evolved into the Revolutionary Agreements. Since that time, Marian has devoted herself to introducing these principles into the lives and work of hundreds of thousands of people throughout the world.

Marian's passion for the principles of authentic leadership and compassionate communication have led her to speak before audiences of thousands; to consult with businesses ranging from mom-'n'-pops to Fortune 100 corporations; to serve on and chair national and international committees and boards for both profit and nonprofit organizations; and to continually search out new avenues and contexts for her pioneering work.

In 2002 she served as the first woman chairperson of the

Mannatech Corporation's peer-elected, ten-member Associate Advisory Council. Prior to this, in 1998, the Mannatech field leadership adopted an early version of the Revolutionary Agreements as their "Leadership Agreements," which now serve a quarter-million active associates worldwide.

Among her pioneering works, Marian co-authored *VisionWorks: Setting Your Sights on Success* (1991, New World Design Center); *The American Team: 7 Steps to Genuine Teamwork in the White House and Beyond* (1992, New World Design Center, and incorporated into *Blueprint for Presidential Transition*, Washington DC); and *Rings of Empowerment* (1993, Global Family). She currently serves as a contributing writer and editor for *Networking Times* and as a coach to private individuals and business leaders nationwide.

To contact the author about
coaching, presentations or workshops,
please send an email to:
marian@revolutionaryagreements.com.

Or call toll-free at:
877-799-2884

Or write to:
Marian Head
P.O. Box 1113
Niwot, Colorado 80544-1113

To receive our free e-letter, with practical applications,
success stories and other exciting news about
Revolutionary Agreements in action, visit
www.revolutionaryagreements.com
and click on
Revolutionary News.

Marlin Press is dedicated to providing
publications and presentations that make a positive
difference in the life of each person we touch.

Please visit our website
to order products and contact us:
www.marlinpress.com

You may also order products by calling toll-free:
(877) 764-2444

Or you may write to us at:

Marlin Press
P.O. Box 1113
Niwot, CO 80544-1113

Special discounts on bulk quantities are available
to corporations, professional associations, congregations,
book clubs, and study groups.

For details send an email to:
groupsales@marlinpress.com
or write to us at the address above.